FLOWING FROM MY HEART

My heart is inditing a good matter: I speak of the things which I have made touching the king: my tongue is the pen of a ready writer.
Psalms 45:1

A Letter By

V. R. FOREMAN

I0080584

Copyright © 2015 by V. R. Foreman
All rights reserved

Flowing From My Heart
by V.R. Foreman

Printed in the United States of America

ISBN: 0692585524
ISBN-13: 978-0692585528

All rights reserved solely by the author. The author guarantees all
contents are original unless otherwise noted and do not infringe
upon the legal rights of any other person or work. All Bible
scripture references, unless otherwise indicated, are King James
Version. No part of this book may be reproduced in any form
without the permission of the author.

Cover Design by:

Marketplace Associates, LLC
Georgia, USA

Book design by Marketplace Associates, LLC.

DEDICATION

*****

To all of my children and your children and their
children. Everything I do is for you.
I love you without end.

TABLE OF CONTENTS

*****

PREFACE

*****

K asey Sa'Miya, My Love. You are my inspiration, my motivation. For you and all my babies to come, this letter came. The words that follow this preamble were penned for you. I was there to experience your entrance into the earth; an angel manifested. You instantly changed my life. My views on life and love changed forever when you came on the scene. Some things became all the more important, and others became all the more irrelevant. Your presence has made me love my children even more – something I did not think was possible. I love you with a love I cannot accurately express on these pages; but throughout your life, you will feel it and know it with certainty.

My earnest prayer and life's mission for you, as it is for all of my children, is that your future is blindingly bright. My desire is that you succeed in every essence of the word and live to see Jesus in the end. The best way for me to describe my aspiration for your life is to borrow the words of the Apostle John in 3 John 1:2, *"Beloved, I wish above all things that thou mayest prosper and be in health, even as thy soul prospereth."*

If it were up to me, you would never feel pain of any kind. You would never lack or suffer at all. But in my maturity, I have come to understand that those things are necessary for us to be like our Savior, Jesus the Christ. I cry now as I write these words and think of your times of pain that I know must come. So, in our talks and through my writings, I plan to do all I can to encourage you. Since you will not be able to pass through this life without sufferings, allow me to help you prepare so that you may suffer well. I cry at your pain, but I also rejoice in the joy and happiness that awaits you. Knowing that your good days will far outweigh your bad days consoles me.

Though this letter was written for your encouragement and support, My Love, it is my hope that it will sustain many others. The topics in this writing are lived by us all. So to every other soul that has decided to crack these pages and absorb their content, I say – Peace and Success to you.

THANK YOU

*****

To My Beginning and My Ending, The Only Wise God My Father, My Lord Jesus The Christ, My Advocate The Precious Holy Spirit of God, you are My Everything. I acknowledge you in all that I do and know that you are totally and completely responsible for any good thing that ever comes from me. Apart from you, I know I can do nothing at all. Thank you, Father.

To every person who utterly broke my heart, I appreciate everything you did. You've been a great benefit to us all. Thank you for pressing out the Anointing in my life and pushing me towards Purpose.

And to the Greatest Picker that Ever Did Pick, My Marvelously Amazing Husband, who inspires me to new dimensions. I am so blessed to have you and grateful beyond words for my privileged position as your wife. Thank you for having and holding me from now until forever.

CHAPTER I

THE ALPHA
God, The Beginning

Whither shall I go from thy spirit? Or whither shall I flee from thy presence? If I ascend up into heaven, thou art there: if I make my bed in hell, behold, thou art there. If I take the wings of the morning, and dwell in the uttermost parts of the sea; even there shall thy hand lead me, and thy right hand shall hold me. If I say, surely the darkness shall cover me; even the night shall be light about me. Yea, the darkness hideth not from thee; but the night shineth as the day: the darkness and the light are both alike to thee. For thou hast possessed my reins: thou hast covered me in my mother's womb.

Psalms 139: 7-13

*****

Lord, you are
Always near, Always concerned, Always faithful, Always true,
Always forgiving, Always renewing, Always good – to me

And you Cover me, you Surround me, you Shield me,
you Watch Over me, from your seat in Glory

You are Everywhere all at once,
Ever-loving, Ever-perfecting,
Ever-present, Never forgetting -
about me
You are Never too busy, Never too late, Never too tired,
Never too far away, Never unfair, Never not there – for me

Everlastingly merciful, Everlastingly gracious, Everlastingly
righteous
Lord, You Are Always and have always been,
Everything I Need

*****

This is where we start. At the beginning. God. My Love, if there is any one thing I could make you understand and leave with you, it is that God loves you, and He is always there. Always. Each day that He extends to you the mercy of life and the grace to live it, He is there to see you through it: ever-present, with all sovereignty, omnipotence, and omniscience. His love is always surrounding you. As the focus text for this chapter so eloquently describes, no matter where you are naturally, emotionally, or spiritually, God always sees you. You will never be outside of His presence.

He has always been there; from the first moment of your wondrous conception in the warm wrapping of your mother's womb, up to this pointedly precise second. He was there at the alpha of your life, crafting, fashioning, designing and preparing you for an earthly arrival. You have the God of the universe, the Creator of all things watching over your very existence. There is nothing that has ever happened or will ever happen that He does not already know about and have in His control. Be confident in that. He is your Source, for everything. Your source is not your job; your family or friends; or even your strength. God is your Source. He eternally and unconditionally loves you like no one else ever could. And when the love of others fails and fades, His love will endure. For God's love is eternal, strengthening, faithful, dependable, gentle, and longsuffering.

You may not always have the love of people, My Love. Those who make you promises and profess their undying loyalty may break them without a second thought. Those who say they will be forever grateful for the things you have done and sacrifices you have made for them may take you and your kindness for granted. The ones who have your blood running through their veins and vice versa may treat you worse than a stranger. Those who proclaim they love God and seem to follow His ways may shock you with the level of hatred they display towards you. Though you have every right to expect it from those near and dear to you, they may not always reciprocate your love. But when the love of many waxes cold, when they utterly break your heart, even if they all turn against you, God always loves you and His love is an unfailing one that endures forever. He wants you to receive His love and love Him in return with all of your heart, soul, and strength. That is not at all an unreasonable request. Is that not what we want from those that we love? We desire that the love we give be accepted; and we want to feel love and devotion in response to ours.

I believe that there are very few pains greater than being rejected by the one you love. I've been in that place of pain and experienced that heartache more than once. Been there, done that, and will probably write a book about it. That kind of rejection creates a deep, lingering, slow-healing wound.

How must God feel when we continue to reject Him after all that He has done for us? He created this planet Earth and its atmosphere and furnished it with everything that we would ever need to enjoy a full, healthy life before He placed us here. A menial, yet identifiable example is that of expecting parents who set up the house and the baby's room preparing for the arrival. They take the time to decide what kind of environment they want for the baby. Should it be Winnie the Pooh or Elephants or Disney or Baseball? They spend what resources they have to design and rearrange the environment of the baby's personal space to make it as welcoming and comfortable as they possibly can. They even go so far as to 'baby-proof' the entire house in preparation to keep the baby safe as he or she grows. They supply all of the baby's needs before the baby comes, down to the smallest details like pacifiers and baby nail clippers. Why? Because they already have such a love for the baby that they do not ever want him or her to go without or be in need of anything. They want to do all they can to ensure there is a safe, healthy place for the baby to live and grow. That is what God the Father did for us. Parents do it to the degree of a room and a house. God did it to the degree of the Universe…all for us!

After the parents do all they can for their child, what if the child decides to reject the parents' love and sacrifices? What if the child elects to turn totally away from the parents and disregard their loving care? How painful would that be for that mother and father? Very.

Look at God. He loved us so much that He created the cosmos just for our sustainment and comfort. It was all for us, My Love. It was all in preparation for our creation. Genesis chapters 1 and 2 tell that story of the Creator, God the Alpha. And then, there is Calvary. He so loved us that He suffered the Passion of the Cross. God gave His only son, Jesus. Jesus gave His very life. How He suffered in agony! How He was afflicted, punished, and tortured; then mocked, scorned, and ridiculed. Crucified. For us. After all He has done, how can we continue to reject His great love and sacrifice? We should love Jesus because He first loved us.

He is Alpha. He always was and always will be. God is He who Was and Is and Is To Come. Before time began, God was. Our finite human minds stop short of the full comprehension of the Creator of All. The scriptures say that without Him, there was not anything made that was made. Before there was anything else, He was. In the beginning, there was God.

In the beginning of your trial, in the beginning of your heartache, in the beginning of your life's storms, there is God. He knows all about it, and He cares. Take comfort in that, My Love. Keep Him Alpha in all that you do; not allowing anything in your life to become more important to you than the Lord, not your family, your money, your career, your ministry…nothing. Put Him in everything that you do, first. Put God first in your marriage at the alpha, and lean on His guidance to help you be the spouse He has called. Give your children back to God at the alpha, and lean on His guidance to help you raise and nurture them. Allow God to direct you to your career path at the alpha, and trust Him to guide you to success for His Glory. And when you are compensated for your labor, give God the tithe at the alpha. For He is Alpha.

Proverbs 3:6 advises us to acknowledge the Lord in all of our ways and then He will direct us in the ways we should go. We make our greatest life mistakes when we fail to acknowledge the Lord first. That failure often results in us making life decisions that place us outside of God's Will and cause us great pain. But in the words of my Amazing Husband, "life is easy" when we stay in the center of God's loving plan. For He is Alpha.

*****

Prayer: Heavenly Father, thank you for your unfailing, undying, everlasting love for me. Thank you for being there from the very beginning of my every situation. You are always aware of those things that concern me, and you care. Help me never forget about you, but to always keep you first in all that I do. In Jesus' name, Amen.

CHAPTER II

THE VALLEY
Walk Through It

Yea, though I walk through the valley of the shadow of death, I will fear no evil: for thou art with me; thy rod and thy staff they comfort me. Psalms 23:4

*****

Roses are not always red
Violets are not always blue
But God's Love for me is everlasting and forever true.

Birds do not always sing
Leaves are not always green
Promises and vows are not always kept,
despite the seal of a ring

People don't always stay like they say they will do
The stories they tell are not always true
Their smiles are not always genuine, some I can't believe
But God's Love never lies; it never leaves

Friends are not always friendly
The sun does not always shine
But God's Love is enduringly mine

Good things don't always last
Bright flowers, sunny days, birds' songs; people and their
promises, stories, smiles and friendship I may not always have.
In this life, I shall have tribulation, and I will much more have
God's Amazing Love for me through it all.
Therefore, I win - Every time.

*****

Psalms 23. What a powerful passage of
encouragement and faith in the provision,
guidance and faithfulness of the Lord, the Loving
Shepherd of our souls. But what is this valley King
David speaks of in verse 4 of the Psalms? He
describes it to be a place so daunting that it looks
like death. Though daunting it may be, David can
walk through it without fear only because his
Faithful Shepherd is right there, guiding and

protecting him along the way. What a Blessed Assurance!

A valley is a landform that Webster defines as a low point between two hills or mountains. One definition depicts it as an elongated depression. And that is just what David means when he uses the term valley to figuratively describe the low, depressing periods of his life.

Yes, David had his valleys; but this was a man who had his fair share of life's high points as well. In addition to multiple victories over cities of armies as a military commander, David also slayed wild animals with little more than his bare hands as a young shepherd boy. He stood alone to brazenly accept the malevolent challenge of a literal giant of an enemy that he defeated with the discharge of one smooth stone, launched by his faith. Perhaps his highest elevation was being Anointed and Crowned as King over God's chosen people of Israel for 40 years. Those were some irrefutable mountaintop experiences in his life.

Between those mountainous seasons of victory, just as Webster described, there were valleys. The depth of King David's valleys seemed to equal the height of his victories. He suffered the sudden illness and death of his infant son and the rebellious behaviors and murderous plots planned against him by his older son. He endured jealousy-inspired, arduous treatment and homicidal intentions at the hands of his leader whom he had loved and served faithfully. His wife ridiculed him. His entire city was ravaged and burned. His enemies kidnapped his wives, as well as the wives of all of his fellow soldiers; and the very men he had fought battles with and defended in wars made violent threats against his life. It appears that the mighty King David spent most of his adult life trying to avoid being murdered – not by enemies or strangers but by those that knew him the best and should have loved him the most. Having knowledge of his story, it seems powerfully fitting that he would refer to those times as "the valley of the shadow of death". Having to bury his beloved child and run for his very life, again and again, how low and depressing those times must have been for David!

Though he was far from perfect, the Bible describes him as a man after God's own heart and one that was wise in all of his ways. This great lover of God suffered profoundly. But in his suffering, he never ceased to honor, praise and glorify God with a grateful heart. It was during those valley experiences that King David wrote the book of Psalms. There he recorded some of the most beautifully genuine songs and words of praise and thanksgiving ever written to God. His suffering drew him to love and trust the Lord even more. For sure, King David knew a little something about walking through the valley.

Understand, My Love, that the valley will come. Our valley experiences are different. Your valley circumstance may be different than King David's, different than mine, but the condition of it will be the same – a low point. If you have not experienced it yet, as our elderly say, keep living. Because as sure as you are reading these words, as long as the Lord sees fit to give you life, you will most assuredly suffer the valley; and like King David (and me), most likely more than once. This chapter is not meant to frighten you. On the contrary, it is intended to prepare and equip you to walk successfully through your valley experiences. My objective is to encourage you with experiential wisdom, revelation, and testimony that if you suffer well, My Love, you will overcome the valley and it will make you better.

It will seem as though negativity happens in waves. Multiple trials, not just one. Not one thing after another as the cliché goes, but one thing on top of another it will seem. The Bible encourages us with these words: *"We are troubled on every side, yet not distressed; we are perplexed, but not in despair; Persecuted, but not forsaken; cast down, but not destroyed"* 2 Cor 4:8-9. This tells us that we can be in the valley and still have victory! So, here is the truth…

The valleys of your life will be sad, and you will be alone at times. Those days will be cheerless and gloomy. They may get very dark. You may feel like you cannot find your way out. It may seem as if you will never feel 'normal' again. In these valley experiences, happiness will be far from you. There will be times, My Love, when your heart will ache undeservedly, people and feelings that convinced you they were genuine will be proven liars. The sun will have to set sometimes, and darkness will come, so will the rain. Life is going to knock the water out of your eyes. But you must learn to count it all joy because it is in those times, as you navigate each obstacle and maneuver each level of pain, that you will learn who you are in Christ and what is truly authentic in your life.

Some valleys will require that you be isolated. Left alone. You may not understand at the time, but it will be necessary for you to be disengaged and distant from familiar, comfortable things so that greater things may be drawn out of you. You will want company, someone to at least call or come by to see you. However, everyone will be going about their lives, which at that time will seem much more interesting than yours. It's not that they do not love you or care about what is happening to you. The fact is, everyone else's world will keep rotating around its axis even when yours has come to a screeching halt. There will be life situations and circumstances that you must endure alone. Even when they are available to call or visit, your loved ones will not be able to endure it for you, no matter how badly they may be willing to. They can encourage you, temporarily help you escape the emotion of it all with laughter and companionship, pray with and for you; but you alone, My Love, must endure and walk through your valley.

You will make mistakes and decisions that will bring you to those days. And sometimes, others will be the cause of your valley. But be of good courage, My Love. Only be strong and of good courage during those days. You will withstand. Those days are temporary, and they will not last.

Remember that God is Alpha. He will be there at the beginning of it and all the way through it. Though you may be physically alone, in your spirit, you will not be alone. As you walk the hard path of your valley, you may not be able to take your friends and loved ones along; but there are some spiritual aides I advise you to allow as your company. These, you should not be without in your valley.

The Word of God. Do not go on a valley journey without God's Word – His written Word, the Bible, and the word He has spoken in your heart throughout your life. Meditate on His word day and night. Hide it in your heart. As the light to our feet and lamp to our path (Ps 119:105), His Word is what lights our way in dark times. His word brings understanding and opens our eyes to the truth of the situation. His Word is true. You may be without a job, no money coming in but bills nonetheless. Those may be the facts, but the truth is that He promised to supply all of your need according to His riches in glory (Phil 4:19). Jesus said in Matthew 6:33 if you seek Him first, everything else will be added to your life. Everyone may have turned their back on you and left you alone without warning. But the truth of the situation is that you are never alone because He promised never to leave you nor forsake you (Heb 13:5). God is with you in the valley. Your life might be looking convincingly bleak and barren as if nothing good could possibly come from it. But the truth of the situation is that He has plans for your life of peace and not evil, of hope and a future to give you an expected end (Jer 29:11). Do not forget His promises to you that He recorded throughout His written Word. Take comfort in them, knowing that they will surely come to pass.

And if you've ever heard the voice of God speak quietly to your spirit, remember it. When circumstances come that seem contrary to what you know you've heard God speak to you, recall that spoken Word. Apply your faith to it in the valley of those circumstances and proclaim its truth. Because it too will surely come to pass. In Isaiah 55:11, God assures us of that by saying "*So shall my word be that goeth forth out of my mouth: it shall not return unto me void, but it shall accomplish that which I please, and it shall prosper in the thing whereto I sent it.*"

You may not be able to feel God's presence at times, but He is your Creator. He will not forget about you. He is always aware of what is happening in your life as the Author and Finisher of your faith (Heb 12:2). He knows the way that you take, and His Spirit will guide you through if you will allow Him to.

The valley is most times full of pain and lack – two things that cause us to be at our weakest, most vulnerable state spiritually, emotionally, and even physically. Our cunning enemy chooses those times to interrupt our path with temptation. We need the Word of God for strength to resist that temptation. Have faith in God's Word. Exercise that faith in your valley and as the songwriter has said "let Jesus lead you, all the way."

Love. Such a wonderful companion to have in your valley. It releases a sweet aroma into not-so-sweet atmospheres. It splashes beautiful, vibrant color into dark, dull places. It turns away wrath and covers faults. It lifts hung down heads and turns frowns upside down. It is the origin of laughter and the main ingredient for every positive thing. Love is a need. Everyone, no matter how negative or loveless they may seem, has a need to receive love and to give it. It is the foundation of our being. We were created in the image of God, who is the very definition of love.

You may not always feel like being bothered with love. You may not always feel like others deserve the love you give, especially in your valley. Nonetheless, you have been created to love. You have been commanded to love. You are obligated to love. Therefore, while walking through your valley – your dark, dismal days – it is vitally important that you fail not to love with every opportunity. The more you give, the more you will receive. You will not always receive it from the same source to which you give it, but you will always receive it. Learn early to love those that harm you. Practice forgiveness here in the valley. Showing and giving love will shorten your valley days. Withholding love will lengthen them.

Wisdom. Be sure to take wisdom with you. Do not abandon her when times get hard. You will need her more than ever then. Separate yourself from foolishness – foolish conversation, foolish people, foolish places, foolish things and foolish situations. Instead, surround yourself, as often as possible, with wise council. God says, "*He who walketh with wise men shall be wise; but a companion of fools shall be destroyed*" Prov 13:20.

Wisdom and knowledge are not the same. Wisdom is the application of knowledge. A person who has information but fails to use it appropriately is a foolish one. Apply knowledge to your situation, My Love. If you do not have the knowledge, seek it out before you make a determination.

Take heed to make wise financial choices and develop wise relationships in the valley. Do not make life decisions out of emotion or distress or ignorance. At those times, your views are tainted and biased. In the words of my Bishop, Dr. Kevin Betton, Sr, Pastor of The Cathedral of Praise Church Ministries, during his sermon titled <u>Death Valley Christians</u>, "Be careful what you pick up in the valley. If it's not something or someone you want with you on your mountaintop, leave it in the valley!" That was one of the most penetrating messages I'd ever heard, and it changed my life forever. Thank you, Sir!

The valley is a temporary place of not-so-good days. The decisions you make in the valley have a high probability of following you long after your departure. As the saying goes "Don't make permanent decisions in a temporary situation". Do not allow your valley-induced emotions to draw you towards a connection to unhealthy people, unhealthy habits or unhealthy spending to provide momentary satisfaction. Be wise still. I have always told my daughters to "be smart and use the brain God gave you." Foolishness, My Love, will most definitely lengthen your valley and may even sabotage your mountaintop. Wisdom will take your hand and show you the shortest route to victory.

Peace. Blessed quietness. Follow Colossians 3:15 and "*Let the Peace of God rule in your heart…*" It should not be left behind in those days. You will find it difficult to stand in times of trouble without peace. Peace in your mind. Peace in your spirit. The power of peace will command chaos and confusion to order. Jesus spoke three small words of peace and calmed a raging sea. Peace will guard your mind against panicked thoughts of desperation. Walk closely with peace in your valley days. Seek solace in those times. Keep your mind steady and sober. I write to you from experience, My Love. It is possible to have peace within even when everything around you is in an uproar.

The Bible says, *"Whatsoever things are true, whatsoever things are honest, whatsoever things are just, whatsoever things are pure, whatsoever things are lovely, whatsoever things are of good report; if there be any virtue, and if there be any praise, think on these things"* Phil 4:8. Count your blessings. No matter how bad things may get, there is always a blessing taking place. It's where the world gets their phrase "Look on the bright side" and "Every cloud has a silver lining." Focus on the Blesser and His blessings. The air you breathe, your faculties, food, clothing, shelter, transportation, the simple "little" things we so often take for granted are reasons to Bless the Blesser. If you keep your mind on Jesus, My Love, He will keep you in His Perfect Peace. Resist the temptation to panic. Surround yourself as much as possible with peaceful, positive people, places, and things. Do not allow chaos in your spirit. You may not be able to control it externally, but you can surely control it internally. Get in the habit now, before the valley comes, of beginning and ending your day with a time of peaceful prayer and meditation. It centers your mind. And that brings us to…

Prayer. Luke 18:1 says '…*men ought always to pray, and not to faint.*" Prayer is our lifeline. It keeps us strengthened. Without it, we may give up because some valleys challenge our very sanity. They can stretch our mental cords to the limit. Make no mistake; not everyone makes it out of the valley successfully, My Love. There are those who have lost their literal minds in the valley; lost their freedom in the valley; lost their very lives in the valley. They were overcome. They fainted.

But prayer is our connection to our Heavenly Father. It is how we commune with Him. We talk to Him, and He talks to us through prayer. It is where we receive the elements of His wisdom, love, peace, and joy. It is a fundamental building block of our relationship with Christ. Earlier, I mentioned that there will be times in the valley when no one will be available for you to talk to; but God will always be there. He never slumbers nor sleeps, and He longs to commune with you. In prayer, we secure direction, solace, vision, understanding, encouragement, strength, comfort, reassurance, validation, revelation, and answers from the Lord. We need that stuff in the valley! We need to hear from God in those times, spend time in His presence and allow Him to guide us.

Jesus tells us in Matthew 21:22 that whatsoever we ask in prayer, believing, we shall receive it. What a powerful promise! Your faith gives you unlimited access to the Omnipotent One. With the faith of a tiny grain of a mustard seed, mountains can be moved according to Matthew 17:20.

We serve a God who hears and answers the cries of His people. Prayer does change things. That is not just a cliché. "*...the effectual, fervent prayer of a righteous man availeth much.*" James 5:16.

Joy. As strange as it sounds, take joy with you in those days. I can hear you asking, "Joy? In the valley of suffering? What could possibly be joyous about the valley seasons of my life?" To answer those questions, first you must understand that joy is not the same as happiness. Happiness is a pleasant emotional feeling experienced for a temporary period of time that is usually expressed outwardly and is based on current situations. Happiness is based on what is "happening" in our lives. Joy is a spiritual delight that takes place inwardly as a result of the faith we have in God's joyous promises for our destiny. Joy has nothing to do with the present and everything to do with the future. Whatever the situation, you can handle it. Joy makes the load lighter.

Proverbs 17:22 reveals that "*a merry heart doeth good like medicine...*" So, make sure you get some healthy doses of laughter in the valley. You may laugh to keep from crying or maybe even laugh until you cry, but laugh. Although pain will leak through your eyes as tears and fill your countenance, your heart can rejoice in knowing God is with you, that He has mapped out your destiny in Him, and that He is working it out for your good future.

Believe me as I write to you, My Love, that you will, from your mountaintop, look back on those dark days of the valley and lift your hands in Praise and Thanksgiving for them. For they serve a purpose. They will make you stronger. They will make you wiser. They will build your character and increase your faith. They will be what push you to your best self. That is what they are designed to do. You will mature in those days. You will learn much about yourself in those days. You will learn about God, people, and life - lessons that will serve you well in your bright future. So, you can take joy in knowing that no matter how it feels or what it looks like, My Love, your valley is good for you. Even though it will not feel good to you, know that it is good for you.

The marvelous thing about the valley is that it is not just good for you, but it will also benefit those connected to you, those watching you and those coming behind you. The valley will qualify you to be able to recognize and identify with others in their valley and use your experiences to encourage, advice and strengthen them as they go through. We do not suffer for ourselves alone.

Oh, no, My Love, the valley is not only for your benefit. It is for the betterment of us all. We suffer so that others might be healed, delivered and strengthened thereby. For this reason, do not forfeit the opportunity to pass on the wisdom that the valley will afford you. You shall help someone to suffer well. You shall help someone avoid a potential fall into the valley because you will freely share the results of your mistakes and misgivings.

What is this valley King David speaks of in verse 4 of the Psalms? The valley is a place of growth that was designed by God specifically for you. Just as He designed the pit for Joseph, the lion's den for Daniel, Goliath for David and the prison for Paul and Silas, your trials are constructed and crafted explicitly for you. They are a set up for God to get Glory out of your life.

This beautiful poesy that follows is a wonderful expression of how the valleys of our life profit us and others:

I asked God to take away my pride
and God said, "No."
"It is not for me to take it away, but for you to give it up."
I asked God to heal my disease,
and God said, "No."
"Your spirit is whole; your body is only temporary.
Through your afflictions, you will learn to help others who also suffer."

I asked God to grant me patience

and God said, "No.
"Patience is a by-product of tribulation. It isn't
granted; it's earned."

I asked God to give me happiness
and God said, "No."
"I give you blessings; happiness is up to you."

I asked God to spare me pain,
and God said, "No."
"Suffering draws you apart from worldly cares
and brings you closer to me."

I asked God to make my spirit grow,
and God said, "No."
"You must grow on your own, but I will prune
you to make you fruitful."

I asked God to help me love others as much as
He loves me and God said,
"Ah...Finally, you understand..."

- Author Unknown

There was a time in my life that I did not
believe it to be true, but now I know with certainty
that there is life on the other side of the valley, My
Love. Thank God that life goes on! It does not
stop when things go wrong. Life as we know it
may stop, but our life does go on. Yes, when that
person leaves or that job ends, life, as it had been,
ceases to exist. Day-to-day life may suffer a drastic
change, but it does not stop. Live through it. Even

if you have to just go through the motions, get up and go through them. Put one foot in front of the other and eventually, you'll walk away from the past and into the future – out of the valley and onto your mountaintop.

*****

Prayer: My God, thank you for the valley seasons of my life. Thank you for always causing me to triumph. I know that you are in control and have already worked things in my favor. Thank you, Lord. Strengthen me in these seasons that I may suffer well and bring you Glory, and I will give you praise from season to season. In Jesus' name, Amen.

CHAPTER III

THE MOUNTAINTOP
The Season of Victory

For I say, through the grace that was given me, to every man that is among you, not to think of himself more highly than he ought to think; but to think soberly, according as God hath dealt to every man a measure of faith. - Romans 12:3

*****

How do I behave on this mountain?
I cannot be reckless, lest I make a move in error and fall
I must be mindful instead, above all
I cannot be careless, lest I lose my footing and slip
I must be rather careful, and preserve an unyielding grip
I cannot be boastful or brash, lest it crumbles under my feet
I must, however, remain humble, gentle, loving and meek
I cannot look down on those climbing without
stretching my hand in aid,
Lest I lean over too far and plummet into the valley,
ever dismayed.

*****

The mountaintop, the victory we gain over valley obstacles and difficulties, increases our faith in God and His Power in our lives. It is proof that the valley is temporary and solidifies our joy in the truth that "…*weeping may endure for a night, but joy cometh in the morning*" Psalms 30:5.

Hallelujah for the mountaintop! Relief from the valley. Oh, what joy and victory you will experience on the top of that mountain! You will have overcome and made it through when you many times thought you wouldn't. Happiness. Gratitude. Relief. The worst will be over, and you will be able to breathe easy again. That same mountain of trials that stood in your way at one time is what God will use to launch you to your life's high points. Not only will you be on the mountaintop; but prayerfully, you will have grown from your valley experience and learned the lessons that were there so that you will also be a better, stronger, wiser you.

On the mountain, you will reap all that you sowed in the valley, the tangible and intangible. Every act of love you performed, every dollar you cheerfully gave, every compassionate service you rendered, every word of encouragement and support you sincerely spoke, every selfless prayer you prayed, you will surely reap it all. Each act of deceit you devised, each malicious move you made, every vengeful plot you planned, every selfish or envious deed you carried out, each act of disobedience you displayed, and the rebellious ways you behaved will also be reaped, indeed. Do not mar your mountaintop experience by behaving poorly in the valley.

Be mindful of all the spiritual companions you walked closely with in your hard days. It would appear that because your situations have changed for the better, that you will not need them on the mountaintop. Quite the opposite is true, My Love. You will need them just the same. All of the comrades that accompanied you through your valley, the Word of God, Wisdom, Love, Peace, Prayer, and Joy, will also serve you as dear friends in your mountaintop season.

The Word of God keeps us grounded in the truth. The truth is, God's grace and mercy make the mountaintop possible, not our money, education, position or who we know. God is the one who graces us with the ability to make the money, the mind to get the education, the skill to get the position and the personality to build relationships and make positive impressions on others. The Lord God alone opens and closes the doors of opportunity in our lives and gives us the capacity to walk through them.

The focus text for this chapter warns against having an exaggerated opinion of our importance, skill or ability. Though the mountaintop may bring with it a high altitude of position, take care not to allow an elevated air of selfdom and audaciously smug attitudes to invade your psyche. The Word of God keeps those prideful characteristics deterred. It keeps us aware of the power of God working through us. It helps us continue to love and lovingly give to others and instructs us on how to conduct ourselves with meekness and humility in all situations. It helps us to resist the unique temptations that exist on the mountaintop. We need the Word of God.

Our time in the valley should enrich us. We should emerge from it much wiser. The wisdom we gain in the valley serves to enhance our mountaintop experience. It aides in our decision making, relationship choices, and future planning for our purpose.

The valley teaches us to appreciate the love of God and others in our lives. It conditions us to be compassionate toward others. Our egression from the valley leaves us with a deeper understanding of what it means to love, the experience of what real love feels like, and the pain that comes with the absence of love. On the mountaintop, we become prime candidates to love others with a pure heart, fervently – because now, we know.

The mountaintop is not the place to stop praying. Do not fall prey to the false perception that the high altitude of your peak position or circumstance makes you close enough to God that there is no need to commune with Him. No, My Love, never will you ever be so high that you no longer need God. Resist the snare of getting comfortably complacent and settled into the happiness of the mountain. You still have a purpose to fulfill.

God elevates you to the mountain. He expands your sphere of influence. In that high place, you are seen and followed by many, though you may not realize it at the time. It is a place of treacherous terrain. Slick, sharp, rocky temptations with jagged edges of enticements and uneven plains of stress and pressure make up its grounds. There are many hazardous allures and mistakes on which to stumble. If you should slip or lose your footing and fall, many others that are holding on to the coattail of your leadership and example will fall behind you. Therefore, we need God's guidance just as much on the mountain as we do in the valley.

"The steps of a good man are ordered by the Lord: and he delighteth in his way" Psalms 37:23. He is still ordering your steps on the mountain, and He reveals them through prayer. His steps for us are safe and secure. At that height, the fall would be great. For that reason, you need sure footing.

Life is a series of mountains and valleys. Be mindful on the mountain, My Love, because like the valley, it is temporary. If the Lord God graces you to live long enough, you will surely find yourself in the valley again. The Bible tells us that *"a man that is born of a woman is of few days and full of trouble."* Job 14:1. So, when God allows you to rise to the height of your mountain, don't dare look down on others who are in their valley. As you look on others, remember where you came from and how you got to where you are. Know that at any given moment, you could be where they are. Take advantage of every occasion to use your valley experiences to reach out and help pull someone up out of theirs.

Ungodly behavior on the mountain can certainly cut your days there short and send you plummeting into the valley. And so, always be grateful and gracious, never haughty or prideful. Do not pass up an opportunity to do good. Always have a heart and hand to help others along their way. Take the lessons you have learned and share them freely with others. Remind yourself "But for the grace of God, there go I".

*****

Prayer: Dear Lord, thank you for my mountaintop experiences. Thank you for bringing me through, giving me victory and always causing me to triumph. Never let me forget that I am nothing without you. Help me to always be an example of your loving kindness and compassion towards everyone. In Jesus' name, Amen.

CHAPTER IV

T HE CHOICE TO FORGIVE
Forgive and Live

So shall ye say unto Joseph, forgive, I pray thee now, the trespass of thy brethren, and their sin; for they did unto thee evil: and now, we pray thee, forgive the trespass of the servants of the God of thy father. And Joseph wept when they spake unto him.
Genesis 50:17

*****

Forgiveness is a kind gentleman
He is never inappropriate and always respectful
Courageous and humble at the same time
Not prideful, but not weak by any means
He lays his jacket down over the messy puddles of hate and
bitterness
He lends his coat of compassion and understanding to protect
from cold actions and words
He pulls out the chair of my heart and allows unconditional
love to have a seat
He opens doors for peace

Forgiveness is such a gentleman
He does not force himself but waits to be invited

*****

If you have not already, I encourage you to familiarize yourself with the story of Joseph that is recorded in the book of Genesis. It is a beautifully encouraging story of forgiveness from which we can all learn.

Joseph's life was filled with mountains and valleys, all set in motion when his brothers, motivated by evil jealousy, carried out a plot that was intended to kill him. He went from being adored and preferred by his father to the bottom of a pit, to being sold into slavery, to being favored and treated benevolently by his master. He was lied on by his master's wife, thrown in prison, and eventually promoted to the second highest ranking ruler over all of Egypt. God's hand was surely guiding Brother Joseph's life because the evil done against him was used as a means to bless him abundantly.

Yes, it all worked out for Joseph in the end; but what about the fact that his flesh and blood brothers conspired to kill him? They took his freedom and subjected him to a life that could have very possibly been filled with nothing but hard labor and torture. They faked his death to his beloved father to hide their evil deed. How painfully difficult that must have been for Joseph. How does a man get past that much hurt and make it to the point of forgiveness? With the help of the Lord. Joseph did it, and so can we.

You must know from the onset that people are fallible. They err. They are many times wrong in their words and actions. Consequently, it is inevitable that along the way, someone you love will hurt your heart. Someone will embarrass you. Someone will deceive you. Someone will speak lies about you and make attempts to defame your character and reputation. Someone will promise to stay but will leave you instead. Someone will dislike and mistreat you for no apparent reason. Some of those people may be casual acquaintances, some co-workers, and some you may not know at all. But some will be family members, intimate friends, even some fellow church members and leaders in your life.

Know now that people who you have loved with all you have, trusted with your life, given to, sacrificed for, and shared with will wound you. There will be ones close to you that you will least expect to do the things that they will do. Some of their actions will be unintentional, but many of them will be purposeful and aimed right at the bullseye of your heart. Their motives will vary. Some will be jealous or envious. Some will be vengeful and strive to make you pay for what others have done against them. Some will form their opinions of you based on the opinions of others. Some will have been offended by you and fail to tell you or give you the opportunity to make things right again. Some were just raised that way and never taught any better. And some, My Love, some will just be inspired by pure evil. But you must purpose in your heart to forgive them - right now. It is a choice you can make before it happens. Choose to forgive people for their wrong. You must will yourself to forgive although you may never hear an apology or a request for forgiveness. Simply because the God of All the Universe forgives us for all of our wrong, we must do the same unto our neighbors. If He forgives, who are we not to?

When an offense occurs, you only have two options. The alternative to forgiveness is unforgiveness. Holding on to unforgiveness will cause you to avoid certain places and people, miss opportunities or forfeit experiences that you cannot regain and ultimately cause you to miss God's Glory. Unforgiveness is poisonous. It will clutter your mind with unproductive thoughts. If it is allowed to linger too long, like cancer, it spreads from your mind to your heart and turns into bitterness. Bitterness can turn into hatred. Hatred set in your heart can lead to dangerous actions. Prisons all over the world are filled with people who chose not to forgive. The cancerous poisons of unforgiveness, bitterness, and hatred, left to fester inside of you can cause physical sickness and disease. Hospitals, doctor's offices, and cemeteries are filled with people who held unforgiveness in their bosom. Bitterness and hatred can creep into your other relationships and disrupt them. Those toxic emotions can make other people in your life, who have nothing to do with the origin of your pain, pay for your past and can eventually push them away. Divorce courts and unemployment lines are filled with people who refused to forgive. Bitterness and hatred can pollute your life and block you from experiencing their opposites - happiness and internal joy. You do not want to live that life, My Love. That life is lonely and miserable.

If we want to be forgiven, we must first forgive. God requires it. Jesus clearly tells us in Matthew 6:15 *"But if ye forgive not men their trespasses, neither will your Father forgive your trespasses."* Remember, My Love, that you are fallible as well. You will offend someone, hurt someone's heart, embarrass someone, dislike someone, and may even deceive someone. You may promise to stay but leave instead. You may do one, or more, or all of these things. Whether your actions be ones of intent or honest mistakes, you will wound someone. One thing is for sure, we all have sinned and fallen short of the Glory of God as the scripture has said and you will one day, several days, most assuredly find yourself in need of the gift of forgiveness. Won't you appreciate forgiveness being there to receive you when you need it? You will need to be pardoned from the wrong you've done, released from the repercussions of your actions and freed from your guilt. You must grant those same things to those who will harm you.

Some incidents will be easy to dismiss. But others will require you to gather some extra love and go into the reserves of your humility to find that forgiveness. Some forgiveness may not be possible in your strength. Some wounds may be so deep that you will need the Holy Spirit to help you forgive, but you must do it. Keep yourself free, My Love. Forgive.

Brother Joseph's life is a wonderful illustration of forgiveness, but Jesus is our perfect example. Remember how He forgave Judas? Judas was one of His disciples, His student. He was one of the closest people on Earth to Jesus. Jesus blessed Judas with power, poured into him, provided for him, shared everything He had with him and the other disciples and what did Judas do? He betrayed Jesus for money. Thirty pieces of silver were all that The Savior's life was worth to Judas. Knowing what Judas would do and what his actions would cause Him to have to suffer, Jesus still permitted Judas to remain close to Him, even at the last Passover supper that Jesus would share with His beloved disciples before His death. Judas was invited to the table. Jesus chose to forgive Judas before he ever betrayed Him.

Look at how The Savior forgave those that lied on Him and persecuted Him. They stole His possessions and sold them right in front of Him. They beat my Jesus into an unrecognizable state, mocked Him, slapped Him, and whipped Him. They pierced His side with a sword, pierced His head with thorns, drove His hands and feet with nails into a wooden cross and put His bludgeoned, battered, bleeding body high on humiliating display for all to see. As they tortured Him in so many different ways, Jesus forgave them. Aloud, from the cross, as He hung in indescribable physical, emotional and spiritual pain, He said, *"Father, forgive them for they know not what they do!"* Luke 23:24. We must remember our Sweet Savior Jesus and choose to forgive.

The love and concern we give to others may be abused, misused, and thrown back in our face; but we, being Jesus Christ's examples on Earth, must lovingly forgive as He does.

*****

Prayer: Father, thank you for your continuous forgiveness of my sins and mistakes. Thank you that you have deemed me forgiven, not guilty because the blood of your Precious Son, Jesus covers me. Thank you that you do not see me as what I've done but as who you created me to be. Now, Father, help me to forgive those who wrong me. Help me to see them as your creation, your people that your son has died for, not my enemy. Have mercy on them, Father, and help me to show mercy and love them despite their actions. With your help, I can do it. In Jesus' name, Amen.

CHAPTER V

TRUST vs. FORGIVENESS
Apply Wisdom

Let not him that is deceived trust in vanity: for vanity shall be his recompense. Job 15:31

*****

Trust is a delicate and fragile thing
Like fine crystal glass, so very precious and rare
So easily broken and difficult to repair

Trust is a strong, secure thing
Like a steel fortress where you can feel safe
So sure and sound when it is in place

*****

Trust is one of the most valuable things we have to give. It is to be cherished because when we grant it to others, it leaves our lives totally exposed. Trust gives others a direct avenue to our heart and the things that we treasure. With the key of our trust, the most vulnerable areas of our unease and disquiet can be unlocked and accessed almost effortlessly. Our most sensitive buttons can be pushed. Our most private matters can be invaded. We become susceptible to suffering.

But despite the dangers, trust is one of the few things that we many times give away automatically. We often take people at their word and believe what we are told until it proves to be otherwise. We tend to give people the benefit of the doubt when we are not completely sure of the facts. But what happens when the trust that we give is shattered? What happens when our trust is taken for granted and misused? What happens when that key of trust is turned into the lock of our heart with enmity or ill will and our uttermost confidences are betrayed?

Our first human response is most often to shut down, collect all the keys from all who hold them and refuse to reissue. Denying access indefinitely or allowing only the bare necessity of entry would seem to fix the problem, right? Wrong. That is not the solution, My Love. Not only does that lock others out of the intimate spaces of our lives, but it concurrently locks us in to be completely alone with our emotions. That is an unhealthy place to be.

I believe that our relationships with others are of most importance to God, second only to our relationship with Him. In Mark 12: 29-31, Jesus says,

> *"...The first of all the commandments is, Hear, O Israel; The Lord our God is one Lord: And thou shalt love the Lord thy God with all thy heart, and with all thy soul, and with all thy mind, and with all thy strength: this is the first commandment. And the second is like, namely this, Thou shalt love thy neighbour as thyself. There is none other commandment greater than these.*

Since the Lord holds our relationships with one another in such high regard, so then should we. This is why forgiveness and restoration are so vitally important. The problem is that trust and forgiveness are frequently coupled together, almost used synonymously.

Some theorists will tell you that unless you restore that broken relationship to its original state, you have not truly forgiven. They will say that when you forgive, you must treat the offender like they never offended you, otherwise, you have not completely forgiven. That philosophy is understandable but not totally agreeable for me. If we are willing to continue to allow the same people to vandalize our lives, in the same way, time and time again, then yes, that viewpoint works. But a more complete ideology that I would offer for your consideration is to restore broken relationships with wisdom.

Wisdom, as we discussed earlier, is applying knowledge. The Bible tells us that "...*wisdom giveth life to them that have it*" Ecc. 7:12. Wisdom preserves our very life by keeping us from the foolishness that would destroy it. Wisdom in relationship restoration is learning from the state of brokenness and what caused it to become broken in the first place and applying those lessons to the relationship moving forward.

There is a well-told story of a man walking in the woods who finds a snake that had been injured by a bird trying to have it for dinner. The man was moved with compassion and took the snake home. He purchased supplies to create a comfortable environment for the snake. He fed it, cared for its wounds and over time, nursed it back to health. One day while the man was feeding the snake, it bit him. He was shocked and asked the snake

"Why did you do that? After all I've done for you, why would you bite me?" and the snake replied, "You knew I was a snake when you found me."

The moral most often taught through this story is that a person is who they are and if you choose to deal with them, knowing who they are, then you get what you get. But, let us use it as discussion material for our current topic.

This caring man had several options. He could have killed the snake in revenge. He could have held on to unforgiveness and kicked the snake out of his life in anger by putting it back outside to fend for itself. He could have restored the relationship to its original state and foolishly continued to care for the snake in the same manner, leaving himself open to be hurt again. Or he could have restored the relationship, learned the lesson the snake taught him and applied wisdom by putting safeguards in place to protect himself from future pain.

I heard a preacher say something in one of his sermons once that I have not forgotten. It was a simple line of advice that was originally spoken by the great Mia Angelo – "When someone shows you who they are, believe them the first time." That statement supports the truth about forgiveness and trust. Do not confuse the two, My Love. Once you have been offended, you must choose to forgive that person. Resist the temptation to hold the offense over their head or continue to make them or others pay for their fault. Understand that they made an error and learn from it. Love them, but it would be unwise to trust them in that area again.

Consider this. If someone should steal from you, wisdom says not to put them in a position to be able to make that mistake with you again. Past encounters have proven that you cannot trust them with your possessions. Leaving your wallet in their presence or leaving them in your home alone would not be a wise thing to do. They have shown you their weakness, so restore that relationship with forgiveness and love them enough not to tempt them in that area. Our focus text for this chapter tells us that if we continue to trust in false, foolish things, those things are what we will get in return. Therefore, My Love, apply wisdom to your relationships.

The Bible instructs us to put our trust in the Lord, not man. We can fully trust the Lord and the promises that He has made to us in His Word. If we do, then when we have been disappointed or offended by people, we will have the grace to forgive because our trust is in the Lord whom we know is our help and our shield. We know that He is faithful to His Word because *"God is not a man that he should lie; neither the son of man that he should repent: hath he said, and shall he not do it? Or hath he spoken, and shall he not make it good?"* Num 23:19. You can always depend on God, My Love. Trust Him to be faithful when others are not. Trust Him to provide for you when others take from you. Trust Him to fight your battle when others come against you. Trust Him to be the friend that sticks closer than a brother when others turn as if they never knew you.

Broken trust takes time and great effort to repair. It takes a painful toll on relationships, often altering them forever. But we should seek to overcome the bitterness of pain with the sweetness of forgiveness and embellish it with the garnish of wisdom. Forgive the offense. Love the person. Learn the lesson. Be wise going forward.

*****

Prayer: Heavenly Father, thank you for the people you have allowed into my life. I understand that they are in my life for a purpose, and I value my relationships all because you have ordained them. As I navigate the relationships in my life, help me always to trust in you, forgive, love, learn and act in wisdom. In Jesus' name, Amen.

CHAPTER VI

DO NOT JUDGE
Out of Jurisdiction

And the heavens shall declare his righteousness: for God is judge himself. Selah. Hear, O my people, and I will speak; O Israel, and I will testify against thee: I am God, even thy God.
Psalms 50:6-7

*****

Yes, she did it. The act was committed.
Yes, he did it. He even admitted it.

I must put down this gavel of a finger I am pointing
Least I be found guilty of contesting God's Anointing

The condition of the heart, which I know not, matters most
My finite mind of opinions could never come close

*****

Judging, criticizing, finger pointing, drawing conclusions. Be very careful. You may think you know all of the sides to the story, but in truth, God is the only one who knows all. Since we do not know, we can in no way accurately judge. To that end, the responsibilities of judgment and conviction belong to God, not us. They are completely out of our area of God-given authority. The scriptures warn *"Judge not, that ye be not judged. For with what judgment ye judge, ye shall be judged; and with what measure ye mete, it shall be measured to you again."* Matt 7:1-2.

The Bible further helps our understanding by telling us to consider ourselves when we deal with our brothers and sisters who have been overtaken in a fault (Gal 6:1). You never know what roads this life will cause you to travel or what path your decisions will lead you down. There may be days when you lift your eyes and ask "How did I get here?" So, instead of looking on others with stern eyes of condescension and condemnation, look with the soft eyes of love and compassion, always remembering that if not for the grace and mercy of God, it could have been you. And although it is not you right now, it could be you or someone you hold dear tomorrow. Given the right fusion of emotions and circumstances, anyone is capable of anything, even you. Would you be willing to face the same treatment you are rendering to others?

The world says "put yourself in their shoes" but there is no way you can accurately do that. No matter how well you know the person or the situation, you could never know the entire story. The "inside" story is hidden from us. What goes on in the inward parts of the accused is critical, even in natural court cases. In a natural court of law, the judge and jurors try to determine the condition of the mind and heart of the defendant at the time the act was committed. Was she sane and in her right mind? Did he understand what he was doing and know that it was wrong at the time of the incident? Was she under extreme mental or emotional distress when it happened? Was this act premeditated? What could have been the motive, the heart's intent, behind the crime? Was she in fear for her life? They take all of that into consideration when deciding the verdict and sentencing. If that much consideration for the internal condition of a person is taken in the natural, how much more in the spirit? All we know is what we have witnessed or been told, but that is not the entire story. There is much information to which we are not privy. The internal workings of a person, their mindset, the condition of their heart, the status of their relationship with God; God only knows. That is why, My Love, God alone is qualified to judge righteously.

It is a spiritual courtroom with the Lord God Almighty in the judgment seat, and the witnesses are heavenly as told to us in Hebrews 12:1, *"we also are compassed about with so great a cloud of witnesses…"* That same scripture reminds us that we have our own race to run, our own sins and faults to address. Our sins may not be the same sins as others, My Love, but sin nonetheless. When we feel compelled to swing the gavel of judgment at our neighbor, what should we do instead?

Pray for deliverance. Restore in the spirit of meekness. Encourage in the things of God. Teach sound doctrine that shows the way to a right relationship with Christ. Share our testimony of deliverance. Love in spite of. We should do those things that edify and build faith in others, not tear it down. For it is not our place to condemn, My Love, nor avenge, only God's. It is only required of us to love always, in word and deed.

*****

Prayer: Heavenly Father, thank you that you have deemed that there is no condemnation to those who are in Christ Jesus and who walk after your Spirit. I acknowledge you as the only Righteous Judge. Help me to resist that temptingly high seat of judgment over my neighbors. In Jesus' name, Amen

CHAPTER VII

TRUE BEAUTY
See Yourself as God Sees You

I will praise thee; for I am fearfully and wonderfully made:
marvelous are thy works; and that my soul knoweth right well.
Psalms 139:14

*****

Beauty
Who determines her existence?
Who decides what she is to be?
She is God's Creation. Should not He?

Where does she begin? Will she ever end?
Who determines her worth? Who sets her boundary?
She is God's Creation. Should not He?

Where is the place that she resides?
Is it external or somewhere in eternity?
She is God's Creation and with Him always her home shall be.

*****

Let us first address the ongoing struggle we
have with physical beauty. It can at times be
difficult for us to psychologically get past the
standard of beauty that society has set before us.
That standard is virtually impossible to achieve
without some alterations. The real truth is that
most of the images portrayed of the standard that
we see on billboards, in magazines and on
television and movie screens are altered in some
way. When you see those images, keep in mind the
aid of what I call "photo props" such as pounds of
makeup, skin tanning, added hair, eyelashes and
nails, enhancing pads, slimming undergarments,
etcetera, etcetera. Print ads are airbrushed to
remove flaws and add smooth, clear texture. Most
public figures (males and females) have been
surgically or chemically adjusted or have
undergone extreme conditions to instantly

metamorphose their physical features into something they have been conditioned to believe is beautiful. When you understand that what you see when you see what you see on display in the media is most often not authentic, you must ask yourself whether or not the standard of beauty that society pushes is real or fantasy. Real or not, the standard has been set. It is what we see all around us.

People spend fortunes trying to change things about themselves that they think do not fit into the societal mold of beauty. I'm always saddened to see desperately unsatisfied women who subject themselves to nose jobs, facelifts, Botox injections, breast and buttocks implants, liposuction and other craziness to change their physical appearance. Plastic surgeons and cosmetic doctors get rich off of unfulfilled women looking to purchase their self-esteem and buy a greater level of self-confidence. What these women do not realize, My Love, is that they are perfect in God's eyes. Every piece of them is exactly the way God intended it to be, and that is true beauty.

You must get past the superficial mindset of this culture and know that you were fearfully and wonderfully made by the Lord just as you are, without all the props and adjustments. There is no one else exactly like you in all of the earth, nor has there ever been, nor will there ever be. You are a designer's original not to be duplicated, an authentic masterpiece worth more than can be measured. I believe one of the greatest insults we could sling at our Creator is to want to be or try to be something or someone other than what or who He has designed us to be. In doing so, we say "God, you messed up, and I'm not satisfied with what you did." How gravely insulting that is to our Lord! Never be ashamed of whom God created you to be and how He put you together. We are His design – His handiwork – His art pieces. We were not created to fit into the mold of what society says beauty is.

Honestly, we all have things about ourselves that we could stand to change. Your nose may not be what you would choose but it is what God purposed for you, and it should be marvelous in your eyes. I always say "How boring would this world be if everyone was walking around looking like me?!" God's variety and the disparateness of His designs are the essences of true beauty. When we exist exactly as God designed us, it adds to the array of artistry that is Creation. Your cheekbone placement, hair texture, the shape of your fingernails, the width of your nose, the color of your eyes, the hue of your skin, the size of your feet and all of your other unique features make the medley of Creation that much more beautiful. Isn't that marvelous?!

Now, let us discuss the most important part of your beauty; that part that never fades – internal beauty. Whether you realize it or not, God has invested in you. You have a specific combination of spiritual gifts, talents, intelligence, physical strengths, character strengths, passions, personality quirks, experiences, education and other distinct idiosyncrasies that belong to only you. You do things differently than everyone else. No one can do the things you do the way you do them, and that is special to God. You are, therefore, more valuable than you understand. Let nothing or no one convince you otherwise, not even yourself.

I once had a bad habit (and still slip back into it from time to time) of saying that I am not creative. I would tell others that they had more creativity in the fingernail of their pinkie finger than I did in my entire body. Then one day, God reminded me that He is the Creator of everything...there is no one more creative than He. He created creativity! And if creation flowed from Him and His Spirit abides in me, then I am what He is. So, I now self-correct when I begin to speak negatively of myself by saying I am not a creative person. I may not express it the way others have been designed to, but I do have creativity flowing through me because the Creator lives in me. God holds all power. If His Spirit abides in you, then you are powerful. Stop claiming weakness and inadequacy. God is all knowing. If His Spirit abides in you, the Bible tells us that He reveals. Stop calling yourself stupid. You have omniscience flowing through you. Everything you need to know, His Spirit will reveal to you.

One of my dearest friends, my eternal brother, has this quote by Lao-Tzu (I believe Mahatma Gandhi has been credited with this quote as well) attached to the end of all of his emails as his signature. It reads,

> "Watch your thoughts; they become your words; watch you words; they become your actions, watch your actions; they become habits, watch your habits; they become character, watch your character; it becomes your destiny."

Amen. Thoughts enter the mind through the gates of the eyes, ears, nose and sense of touch. When they are allowed to linger, they leave the mind, move into the heart and awaken emotions. Emotions work their way out of the heart and release themselves into the atmosphere through the mouth as words. Once spoken, those words are given life, as stated in Proverbs 18:21, *"Death and life are in the power of the tongue"*, and they become alive in actions. Actions committed long enough morph into habits and behaviors. It has been studied that anything done consecutively for 21 - 40 days becomes a habit. These habits and behaviors shape your character that consequently, formulates your destiny. So, you see, My Love, it all starts with the thoughts you have about yourself, whether they be positive or negative. The

Bible tells us that "...*out of the abundance of the heart, the mouth speaks.*" Matt 12:34b and "*For as he thinketh in his heart, so is he...*" Prov 23:7a. When I thought of myself as not being creative, I spoke it and canceled out the creativity in me, effectively blocking it from manifesting because of my unbelief. Do not make that mistake, My Love. You must see yourself the way God sees you, fearfully and wonderfully made in His image!

Identify your uniqueness and appreciate it because if you do not value yourself, no one else will. Know your worth. Accept it and embrace it. Treat yourself as valuable and others will do the same. And if they don't, they have no place in your life. Move on. I heard Bishop T.D. Jakes of the Potter's House in Dallas, Texas, say on one occasion that "you have to teach people how to treat you." That statement is the gospel truth! People will do what you allow. They will treat you exactly how you let them. If you set no boundaries in your relationships, others will take liberties with you based on how they feel, not how you feel.

You must know and remember how much God your Creator values you. He has deemed you royal, exclusive, chosen and unique. That is who you are. He has placed a treasure of spiritual gifts and natural abilities inside of you. You were not a mistake by far, MyLove. You may have caught your parents by surprise, but God was the orchestrator of the entire event. Read Jeremiah

1:5, 29:11 and Romans 8:29-30. Oh, how much thought and planning and preparation the Creator put into creating you! You have been methodically molded, carefully crafted, and meticulously made.

God has already placed His seal of approval on you, so you do not have to look to others for validation or justification of who you are or what you are worth. The approval of people feels good to our egos and adds to our confidence, but the absence of it should not subtract from that confidence. You will not always meet the approval of others. Many times, people will disapprove of some aspect of you, though they may never tell you. They may discount you and your abilities or fail to acknowledge or appreciate your efforts and contributions. Prevent yourself some unnecessary heartache and purpose not to please people. In all that you do, do as unto the Lord, not man. Seek to please God in every area of your life because Heaven holds our reward, My Love, not man.

Understand that when others reject you, walk away from you or turn their back on you, it is because they do not see or understand your value. Do not let that cause you to doubt it. Not everyone is meant to be with you for the long-run. There are those that are only meant to pass through your life. Their assignment is to teach you something about yourself, about God, or about life. Then there are those that come to stay, to walk your journey with you with love and encouragement for the duration. When you belong to God, nothing that happens in your life, My Love, is happenstance. There is a reason for every situation. God has ordained your steps and each one has a purpose. He is the Author, the Alpha. He orchestrates all that goes on in the life of His people. When others disregard you, it is not a coincidence. Learn the lesson they came to teach you and move on with those that are with you for a lifetime.

One lesson I have lived and learned through much pain and many tears is that you cannot make someone love you back. You cannot love them enough. You cannot please them enough. You cannot tolerate enough of their hurtful actions or meet enough of their unreasonable demands. No matter how hard you try, how much you give, or how deeply you compromise your worth, you simply cannot make someone love you back. Save yourself from that torturous ache. Never try to force a relationship. True relationships happen naturally, on their own. You do not have to try to prove that you are worthy of love or make people see your value or your beauty. It shines through on its own. Those that are meant to be in your life, they see it. You do not have to force it on them. Just be your naturally beautiful self.

*****

Prayer: Heavenly Father, thank you for my life. Thank you for the beauty that you've given me inside and out. Help me to make this world a better place by being exactly what you've created me to be. Help me to see myself the way you see me — fearfully and wonderfully made in your image — beautiful. In Jesus' name, Amen.

CHAPTER VIII

T HE BUTTERFLY
Nature's Radiant Revelations

Therefore, if any man be in Christ, he is a new creature: old things are passed away; behold, all things are become new.
2 Corinthians 5:17

*****

Spread Your Wings and Arise

There are times in our lives
We feel much like
A flower struggling to bloom;
We go through those times of change and growth
Like a caterpillar in a cocoon
Nobody can see the Lord's hidden work
Until the day we break through —
Then we can begin to spread out our wings
And arise as butterflies do
God has a much higher calling for us
And wants us to rise up in Him;
We can make such a difference
If we'd only realize the potential we have within
So allow the Lord to work in your life,
To make you all you can be —
So you will one day be able to soar
And know what it means to be 'FREE.'

© By M.S.Lowndes

*****

There is a reason God created what He created the way He created it. We can learn so much about our Creator by simply studying His beautiful creation. Consider the delightful butterfly. I love them; not just for their grace and beauty but also because of what they reveal about God and our lives as Christians. They are a beautifully symbolic realization of the focus text for this chapter. When we become born again and accept Jesus as our Lord and Savior, our lives are characteristically parallel to that of a butterfly. His love and guidance transform us into the creation He has destined for us to be.

The radiant butterfly begins its life journey as a tiny worm-like creature called a larva. Larvae are very tiny, like our faith when we become born again in Christ. The larvae's primary mission in life is to eat and grow. They grow very rapidly, shedding their old skin along the way. When we are new in Christ, we must feed our faith so that it may grow. We feast on God's Word, written and spoken, and fellowship with His people, the Church. The Bible says "...*faith cometh by hearing, and hearing by the Word of God*" Ro. 10:17. So that we may hear His Word, God has given gifts to the Church in the form of Pastors, Teachers, Evangelists, Prophets, and Apostles "...*for the perfecting of the saints, for the work of the ministry, for the edifying of the body of Christ*" Eph. 4:12. As we hear the Word, grow in our faith and become more like Christ, like larvae, we shed as well. We cast aside ungodly habits, ill behaviors, bad attitudes, and sinful thought processes.

Eventually, larvae mature into caterpillars. At this stage of life, the caterpillar creates a cocoon-like covering for itself and rests therein. Alone. This is where the renewal happens. I imagine it to be a bit painful for the caterpillar because inside this covering, everything about it changes. Its tissues, limbs, and even its organs change. When it finally emerges from the covering, nothing about it is the same. It is a totally new creature. As Christians, we also encounter cocoon-like experiences, which we discussed earlier. We called them valleys, those painful, alone times that produce beneficial change.

The caterpillar emerges from isolation into its final stage of maturity, a butterfly. Free from the cocoon, the butterfly's old life of crawling around on its belly, chewing on rough leaves for nourishment is over. It now flies high above its old habitat and way of life, covering large areas, from beautiful flower to beautiful flower feasting on the sweet nectar they hold. It no longer looks the same, moves the same, or eats the same. Everything is new! Now, in its most exquisite state, it begins to live out its true purpose, to pollinate. As it flutters from one radiant flower to the next, it fertilizes them by spreading the pollen necessary for the flowers to grow and reproduce, thus, stimulating the generation and expansion of nature's beauty. Isn't that marvelous?!

So are our lives in Christ, My Love. It is only after we accept Jesus and His gift of salvation that we truly begin to live out the purpose for which we were created. As we dine on the Word of God and mature in Him, He empowers us with His Spirit while we encounter one precious soul after another, pollinating their lives with His love and reproducing souls for the Kingdom. Through the wisdom and guidance of the Holy Spirit, we fertilize the souls of others with the pollen of

God's Word, making disciples of men. What Glory that brings to our King! Oh, how He is esteemed when His creation operates as He has designed! The Bible says that men will see our good works and glorify our Father, which is in Heaven (Matt. 5:16). Simply amazing.

The transformed life of a butterfly is such a vivid, lively example of God's power to convert. It has one life, goes through a metamorphosis, and then has a totally new life with no similarities of its former existence. The butterfly is 2 Corinthians 5:17 in action. Empowered by the blessings of God's grace and favor, we as His people can soar into our Divine Purpose.

The life cycle of the lovely butterfly is only one display of the workings of God's plan and order that He shows us through His glorious creation. There are many others. The Bible encourages us to watch nature and take note.

Unassuming things such as the quarterly changing of the seasons remind us that no season in our lives lasts forever. We will have some cold, wintery seasons of labor without reward, some spring-like seasons of growth, some wonderfully enjoyable summer-like seasons and some autumn-like seasons of reaping from the seeds of our labor. They are all temporary. Rainfall is necessary for growth in nature just as it is in our lives. We all love bright, sunny days, but too many of them would destroy the earth. Rain, although it is gloomy, dismal and it restricts our activities, it refreshes the earth and prepares it for growth. It is necessary. As it also is with the sad, murky days of our lives. They are necessary for our spiritual growth and character development.

Proverbs 6:6-8 states *"Go to the ant, thou sluggard; consider her ways, and be wise. Which having no guide, overseer, or ruler, provideth her meat in the summer and gathereth her food in the harvest.* This directive by God is a fantastic example of how He expects us to guard against slothfulness and poor planning. If you ever study the life of an ant, you will find him to be a forward-thinking co-laborer, who is far from lazy. Jesus also told the disciples,

> *"Behold the fowls of the air: for they sow not, neither do they reap, or gather into barns; yet your heavenly Father feedeth them. Are ye not much better than they?...and why take ye thought for raiment? Consider the lilies of the field, how they grow; they toil not, neither do they spin…wherefore, if God so clothe the grass of the field, which today is and tomorrow is cast into the oven, shall he not much more clothe you…?"*
> Matt 6:26, 28, 30.

What a wonderful reminder that the Lord will undoubtedly provide for us!

Pay attention to nature, the seasons, how things grow, develop and flourish, and you will gain wonderful revelation into the mind of our Creator.

All of Creation testifies of the Power, Majesty, Brilliance and Beauty of our God!

*****

Prayer: Heavenly Father, My Creator, thank you for the beautiful revelations of yourself that you have placed all around us. Help me not to live life so fast-paced that I fail to take the time to pay attention to, learn from and enjoy your creation which you have placed here for me. In Jesus' name, Amen.

CHAPTER IX

G IVE
Live Like a River

Every man, according as he purposeth in his heart, so let him give; not grudgingly, or of necessity: for God loveth a cheerful giver. 2 Corinthians 9:7

*****

Give, give, give
Give it in Jesus' name
Give, give, give
Give it in Jesus' name
Give, give, give
Give it in Jesus' name
And the Lord will bless you real good!

Author Unknown

*****

My favorite Deacon often sings that little melody as he stands in front of the church holding the offering basket. It is always a delight to hear him because singing is not one of his God-given talents! As I think of giving in any form, I can hear Deacon Allen's deep voice singing "Give it in Jesus' name, and the Lord will bless you real good." Most of the time when we think of giving, we think of finances. We think about giving our money because usually when someone talks about giving in an organized setting, they are talking about money. But giving goes far beyond our wallets, My Love.

"Live like a river" has become my life's motto. I read that phrase while studying the book <u>The Blessed Life: The Simple Secret of Achieving Guaranteed Financial Results</u> written by Pastor Robert Morris. No matter how much the rains fall and fill their banks, rivers never overflow because their water continuously flows out into the sea. I desire to live my life in the same manner. Whatever resources God provides, I want to release them continuously to God's purposes.

Genesis 8:22 states that *"While the earth remaineth, seedtime and harvest…shall not cease."* You will surely reap a harvest from the seeds you sow. Hindus and Buddhists call it karma. Some people refer to it as kismet. Others simply say what-goes-around-comes-around; but the Bible calls it sowing and reaping – *"Be not deceived; God is not mocked: For whatsoever a man soweth, that shall he also reap"* Gal 6:7. And whatsoever means just that, whatsoever. As we established earlier, we reiterate here, if you show love, you will receive love. If you give money, you will receive money and provision. If you lend your support, you will receive support. If you sow anger, you will receive anger. If you sow deceit and backbiting, those are what you will receive. Again, you may not receive it from the place where you sow it, and you may not receive it at the time you sow it; but I echo that you can rest assured, My Love, that of the seeds you have planted, you will surely reap a harvest. Not only will you reap; but your harvest will always be more than your seed. I heard someone say that when you sow an apple seed, you reap an apple tree! So true.

I have come to find, My Love, that there is always an opportunity to give, and we always have something we can give. Even if it is not what is asked of us, we always have something to give. The Bible tells of a story in Acts chapter 3 that is a wonderful example of that fact. The Apostles Peter and John were going to the temple to pray and worship God when they were met at the gate by a man who was crippled and could not walk. The man asked the apostles for money just as he did of everyone who passed his way. Peter's response to the man's request in verse 3 was *"Silver and gold have I none; but such as I have give I thee: In the name of Jesus Christ of Nazareth rise up and walk. And he took him by the right hand, and lifted him up: and immediately his feet and ankle bones received strength."* The man asked for money but what he really needed was healing for his spirit and body. Peter helped him get what he needed, and now he had the strength and ability to get what he was originally asking for by making his own money. Hallelujah! In that brief moment, Peter gave his love and compassion, his time and attention, and his energy all while sharing his faith. How wonderful! It only takes a moment to give, My Love. And the most powerful gifts we can give last much longer than money.

There is an old saying that states: If you give a man a fish, he can eat for a day, but if you teach him how to fish, he can eat for a lifetime. Material things, although important and necessary, many times only bring temporary relief. But intangible, irreplaceable giving of genuine loving care and concern, time and shared faith and knowledge accomplish far more and bless more than just the person to whom it is given. If someone would choose not to just satisfy the hungry man's immediate need with one fish sandwich but to show concern instead and take whatever amount of time and care needed to pour knowledge and skill into his life, the man will be empowered to not only feed himself but his entire family. He could also teach others the skills to feed their families for generations to come; thus delivering him and everyone connected to him from hunger perpetually. What a wonderful feeling to know that just a little bit of your time could positively impact someone's future forever!

Aim always to be ready and willing to give cheerfully, not grudgingly. Give as much as you can as often as you can. Look for opportunities to deposit generously into others, not just your material substance but your very essence. Share your time, your love, your encouragement, your support, your knowledge, your skills and most of all, your faith. The more you receive, the more you should give out. God chooses to bless us so that we can turn and be a blessing to others. And in blessing others, we are blessed all the more.

*****

Prayer: My Gracious Heavenly Father, thank you for being so good to me. Thank you for the manifold blessings you continue to bestow on me and my family. As you have so freely given to me, help me also freely give. As I strive to be more like you, Jesus, help me always to be in a position to give generously to others. You gave your all for me, help me to do the same for your Glory. Thank you, Father. In your son Jesus' name, Amen.

CHAPTER X

CHANGE
The Consistency of Change

*To everything there is a season, and a time to every purpose
under the heaven: A time to be born, and a time to die; a time to
plant, and a time to pluck up that which is planted; A time to
kill, and a time to heal; a time to break down, and a time to
build up; A time to weep, and a time to laugh; a time to mourn,
and a time to dance; A time to cast away stones, and a time to
gather stones together; a time to embrace, and a time to refrain
from embracing; A time to get, and a time to lose; a time to
keep, and a time to cast away; A time to rend, and a time to*

sew; a time to keep silence, and a time to speak; A time to love, and a time to hate; a time of war, and a time of peace.
Ecclesiastes 3:1-8

*****

My God, I accept your Sovereignty.
Whatever your Will, let it be.
Have your Divine Way in me.
What you have purposed for me, I will be.

With your help, I will obey and do your Will.
Come what may, help me to be still.

Father, your Kingdom come.
Lord, your Will be done.

*****

You've probably heard all the old familiar adages about change like, "change is inevitable," "all good things must come to an end," "nothing lasts forever", and "ride the wave of change, or you will drown." The concept of those sayings is correct. One thing you can count on is that things will change. Seasons change. People change. Change can be uncomfortable. Change can be inconvenient. Change can be confusing and downright scary. But if you protest and become rigid and resistant, you will only prolong the inevitable because you cannot stop it. It will happen. Aside from God's love for you and His Word, change is the only constant in this life. Eventually and many times when you least expect it, change will come.

Everything evolves. People, relationships, jobs and careers, technology, ideas, the universe itself. All of creation is ever evolving and changing, consistently. It would behoove you, My Love, to not ever allow yourself to get too comfortable and settled into anything. Always be open to change and embrace it when it comes.

People change and evolve because as life goes on, it brings different experiences and exposure to various things that have an impact on our thought processes, belief systems, values, priorities and overall understanding and knowledge concerning life in general. People are ever learning through their experiences. Consequently, our behaviors and characteristics and habits will reflect those life lessons. Twenty-year-old single college students have totally different mindsets, ideologies, and priorities than thirty-year-old married adults. The priorities and mindsets of a thirty-year-old married adult without children are very different than those of a thirty-year-old married adult parent or a twenty-three-year-old single parent or a sixty-five-year-old retiree or an eighty-year-old widow. And so, because people do change, their relationships do also. Their responses and reactions to things, the way they interact with others, the way they view life and love, conflict and resolution, money and possessions; it all changes over time.

Oh, how miserable life can be when we do not accept the imminence of change! We should change with change. Although, we do have a choice. Rather than welcome the change, we could insist on remaining the same. We could decline to accept that the change is from God and a part of His sovereign plan for us. We could complain the whole way. We could even determine in our heart to have a bad attitude and harbor anger about the change. If we make any of those negative choices, we then thwart the blessings that accompany the change. Because for the Child of God, He works it all for the good. Whatever the change He permits, it includes a blessing. As we mentioned earlier, nothing in the life of a Child of God is happenstance. It may catch you by surprise, but you must know that God knew well beforehand, and He allowed it to be. Accept His sovereignty. No, My Love, you will not always understand and you most definitely will not always agree but you must accept the sovereign Will of God. Bishop Betton always teaches that "Comprehension is not a Prerequisite for Cooperation". God does not require that you understand, but He does require that you obey.

The Sovereign and All-Wise God holds the seasons of change in His hands. When those seasonal winds begin to blow in your life, resist the temptation to rebel and complain; but instead, *"In everything give thanks: for this is the will of God in Christ Jesus concerning you." 1 Thess 5:18.*

*****

Prayer: Heavenly Father, thank you for your Will being performed in my life. I acknowledge your Sovereignty, but I need your help to always accept it – without complaint or reluctance. You know what is best for me. Help me to yield totally to your way. In Jesus' name, Amen.

CHAPTER XI

NO MORE FEAR
Love is the Answer

There is no fear in love; but perfect love casteth out fear: because fear hath torment. He that feareth is not made perfect in love.
1 John 4:18

*****

Fear is the enemy of Faith
One of the most dangerous 4-letter words is he
So small and deadly

He kills dreams and buries success
Many visions he has suffocated to death

He carries failure and grief
He is fed by our unbelief

Fear is a choice
Choose to defeat him with the spoken Faith of your voice!

*****

Confession time. They say it is good for the soul, and I totally agree. So, I confess that it took me an unnecessarily, inexcusably long time to do the things that God had assigned me to do. Why? Public Enemy #1 – Fear. God had invested gifts, talents, education and experiences in me that He wanted to be used for a specific purpose. I knew that, but I was terrified. And so, I procrastinated. I successfully alluded, avoided and doggedly dodged my purpose. I allowed entirely too many distractions to divert my attentions and take up my time. I sat spiritually dormant for years. That is a hard thing to write and expose to the world, but I can own it now. I was guilty of making it look like I had my life together while my spirit was all out of whack. I started spinning my wheels with busy work because it made me feel useful, like God was pleased. All Lies. I was running and hiding from the demand of my purpose. As long as it did not challenge my ability or knowledge, I would do it. I served on the usher board, sang in the choir, worked in the administration office, managed the church bookstore, served on the Trustee Board, taught Sunday School, served as the Sunday School secretary, served as the Women's department secretary, served on my pastor's business committee, danced with the dance ministry and flagged with the flag ministry while simultaneously raising four children, working a job and running a household. It was a sad state of affairs. At the root of it all, I was full of fear. I would start towards my purpose, but it would get challenging, so I would stop and place my focus elsewhere.

This went on until one of my eternal sisters who was living in another country at the time texted me out of the blue one day and asked the simple question, "What aspirations do you have, but yet they seem unobtainable?" It instantly brought tears of regret to my eyes. I knew the answer immediately. I knew what I wanted to do. I knew what God had equipped me to do. He had aligned my education up with it starting in high school when my mother refused to send me to an ordinary public school and submitted my application to the Business Magnet High School in the downtown area of our city. He had confirmed it through my college English instructor who asked if he could use my first short story as an example for all of his other classes to follow. He confirmed it through the Army First Sergeant who was so impressed with the counseling statements that I had written for the soldiers, that he would post them on the company wall as examples for all other non-commissioned officers to follow. He confirmed it through my Pastor who would bring me his college essays, reports, doctoral thesis and even the draft for what he intended to be his first published book for my proofreading and editing input. He confirmed it through my Amazing Husband who insisted I copyright a poem that I scribbled out of my head one day sitting at my desk at work. I knew that God had given me the ability to write. I knew that God had given me an entrepreneurial spirit. But I was petrified. Completely paralyzed by fear. So many ambitions He had placed in my spirit, but not one did I have the courage or confidence to pen or fully pursue. The real truth behind my fear was that I could not see myself successfully accomplishing anything. I could not see myself doing the things that had been shown to me and prophesied over my life. I wanted to, but my mind would not stretch that far.

God spoke through my eternal sister. "What aspirations do you have but yet they seem unobtainable?" That was not my sister asking, that was God reminding me that He Himself had given me those aspirations. He had given me the desires of my heart. He had placed them there. He continued to use my eternal sister through an email she sent the very next day with the subject title "No More Fear". In the email, God used my sister to say,

> "Are you secure in who you are in Christ and who He is in you? If so, then do NOT be afraid of what might happen...fear holds you back, and God needs you to move forward. You are adequate, you are bold and confident, and you are beautiful, you just have to believe it! God tells you to go, but you are afraid – no more fear! It's time to get it embedded so deeply in your spirit that when the enemy attempts to attack, God slaps him in the face with His plan and His purpose for your life. His plan is devised to elevate you in the midst of your imperfections, but fear MUST flee, and it's up to you to get rid of it...say it – write it – leave it – be it – He has equipped you to just do IT! Nothing you do catches Him by surprise. His plan accounts for your failures and mistakes, but the test is will you allow these temporary obstacles to further delay His purpose for you and continue to willfully walk in disobedience? When you KNOW what God has called you to do, created you to do for His glory but yet you do nothing – hard truth, it is disobedience."

Disobedience? She had stepped on my spiritual toes! Did she have to say it like that? *DISOBEDIENCE???* I had not realized that I was walking in disobedience, but she was right. That is exactly what I was doing. That email changed my life forever. Thank you, Big Sis! When that truth jumped off of the computer screen and hit me in my spirit, it was a hard pill to swallow. I could only repent through my tears and thank my Heavenly Father for chasing after me, for not giving up on me, for yet trusting me with His purpose and assignment.

I admit that I still regret all of the time that I let pass through my life as I sat idly. My Love, do not let this be you. When God reveals to you what His purpose for your life is, run after it. Do not hesitate. Forbid fear to invite intentional procrastination and willful distractions to accompany you on your life's journey.

As the focus text for this chapter so plainly states, fear does indeed have torment. It invades your mind with haunting thoughts of inadequacy, rejection, disapproval, criticism, and failure. But perfect love casts out fear. Thank the Lord! His perfect love for us and our mature, uninhibited, complete love for Him leaves no room for fear. It empowers and motivates us to honor Him with our lives and live out the purpose that He has revealed to us.

After I read my sister's email, God placed that scripture in my spirit "…*but perfect love casteth out fear.*" That night, and the next morning, I meditated on that phrase and began to ask God for a greater revelation of the scripture. I needed Him to help me understand what perfect love is and just how it could cast out my fear. I meditated on that scripture and decided to ask my Amazing Husband what it meant to him, and he reminded me of an incident that had happened years earlier. Though he had not been there when it happened, He recounted with great accuracy an occurrence I had told him about involving my third daughter when she was a little girl.

She was playing outside, and the front door of the house was open so I could see her through the screen. After some time, I walked by the window and caught a glimpse of her in the front yard. She had a look of pure terror on her face. I hurried to the screened door and saw her standing there frozen in mid-stride. I followed the gaze of her eyes and saw that between her and the front door was a huge growling, snarling, foaming stray dog daring her to make a move. Their eyes were locked on one another. My daughter was so frightened that she could not make a sound. She was just fixed there, silent tears sliding down her trembling cheeks. The dog was ready to attack. Without hesitation or weapon of any kind, I ran out the door full speed ahead straight for the dog. I yelled at the top of my lungs commands for him to leave my yard or else; and I meant it! That dog was going down. I had every intention of doing what it took to get my child in the house unharmed; whatever the cost, even if it meant my life. I believe that animal knew that he did not stand a chance against me at that moment, and he made the wise decision to run for his life. As my Amazing Husband retold the story that day, I remembered those emotions and realized that it could have been a grizzly bear threatening my daughter that day, and it would not have mattered. My actions and my intentions would have been the same. She was the object of my love, and there was simply no way I could have let her be harmed, especially when I had the power to prevent it.

God, through my Amazing Husband, was using the analogy of that life experience to answer my prayer and reveal to me what perfect love is. My daughter needed me. She depended on me to do something, and my love for her was not going to let her down even though the odds were stacked high against me. My love for her removed all the fear that I normally would have had under other circumstances. Perfect love is when we love uninhibitedly, without selfish reasons or any regard for ourselves. Perfect love is not about us at all. It is about the object of our love.

Jesus is our perfect example. Look how His perfect love for the Father drove Him to walk out His purpose, whatever the cost. His assignment to die for the sins of the whole world came at an extreme price. How He suffered for the object of His love! When we love God with all of our heart, soul, and might, it casts out the fear that would otherwise keep us from doing what He needs us to do, which is to walk out the purpose for which He created us. Our perfect love for God will mean more to us than whether or not people accept our gifting, like our talents, agree with our visions or approve of our dreams. His perfect love for us will overcome any disappointments and even failures that may come during our sojourn and cause us to endure until our purpose is complete.

My Love, I allowed fear to waste far too much of my time. Please learn from my life lessons. Trust God and know that if He has purposed you for it, He has also equipped you for it. He will give you what is needed to bring your purpose to pass, whether it be knowledge, ability, finances, connections or other resources. He will be your complete source. Where your abilities end, His will begin. Trust Him. Do your very best and God will do the rest.

Let us end this chapter of fear, not only in this letter but in your life. The following writing is an excellent expression of what happens when we cast fear out of our minds. I first came across it in the movie <u>Akeelah and the Bee,</u> and I loved it even though at that time, I did not fully embrace its message. But I pray, My Love, that you will.

OUR DEEPEST FEAR
By, Marianne Williamson

"Our deepest fear is not that we are inadequate.
Our deepest fear is that we are powerful beyond measure. It is our light, not our darkness that most frightens us.
We ask ourselves, "Who am I to be brilliant, gorgeous, talented, and fabulous?"
Actually, who are you *not* to be? You are a child of God. Your playing small does not serve the world.
There is nothing enlightened about shrinking so that other people won't feel insecure around you.
We are all meant to shine, as children do. We were born to make manifest the glory of God that is within us. It's not just in some of us; it's in everyone.
And as we let our own light shine, we unconsciously give other people permission to do the same.
As we are liberated from our own fear, our presence automatically liberates others."

*****

Prayer: Heavenly Father, thank you for investing in me. Show me clearly the purpose that you have designed me for and help me to use all that you have placed inside of me to bring you pure glory. For I know that without you, I am nothing. But through you, I believe I can do all things. In your son Jesus' name, Amen.

CHAPTER XII

PROCRASTINATION
Postponed Purpose

I must work the works of him that sent me, while it is day: the night cometh, when no man can work. John 9:4

*****

The bread of idleness is an expensive taste
It costs my priceless time
Time so precious that I must no longer waste
But use for my Purpose Divine

*****

We previously discussed how God has placed purpose and destiny in the plan of our lives. We've already stated how He has equipped us with the gifts, talents, intellect and characteristics we need to accomplish His plan for us and through us. He has done His part. We must do ours. He has formulated the plan. We must work the plan. We can go back to the previously referenced verse of scripture in Jeremiah 29:11 where the Bible specifically tells us that God has a plan for our lives. We can go to the scriptures in Ephesians 1:11 and Romans 8:28-30 where we learn that God has always known us and has predestined us. He has the plan for our lives, and our passions and abilities point to His plan.

If you are unsure of His plan for you, seek Him diligently for it. And as you petition the Lord for the blueprint of your life, let me offer a few questions for you to consider: What are you better at than anything else? What are you passionate about? When you operate in or around the thing that you are passionate about, does it give you a sense of satisfaction? Would you do it for free and still be happy doing it? If you can answer those questions, then you have the clues to your destiny.

You see, My Love, God has already laid out this often confusing and chaotic life for us. All we have to do is trust Him and follow His guidance. He saves us from just wandering aimlessly through our existence with trepidation about what to do with our lives. What a gift He has given each of us – the gift of Purpose.

Purpose is accompanied by the blessed gift of Time; time to fulfill our Purpose to the best of our abilities for the Glory of God the Father. My Amazing Husband once said during one of our quiet conversations that "the essence of a person is their time." That being true, when someone gives you their time, whether it is to do something specifically for you or to be specifically with you, they are giving you their very best. Always be grateful for it and never take it for granted.

Time is precious, My Love. So precious because once it has passed, it cannot be recommenced. Spent time cannot be regained. It is lost forever, and any good economist will tell you that scarcity creates value. Our time, My Love, is limited, hence a most valuable commodity. It is numbered. It has an end and will one day be no more for us. And though we know that it will end, we do not know when. The next second of time is not guaranteed to us. James 4:14 says *"Whereas ye know not what shall be on the morrow. For what is your* life? *It is even a vapour, that appeareth for a little time, and then vanisheth away."* Time is indeed invaluable. The passing of it is irreversible. As the focus text for this chapter so simply states, the amount of time we have to accomplish Purpose will not last forever...." *the night cometh, when no man can work"...* Oh, to stand before the Judgement Seat of the Creator God having no answer to how we spent all opportunities, gifts, talents and resources He freely gave. What degradation for our souls! What dishonor to Our Lord! Therefore, MyLove, the gifts of Purpose and Time must be respected, not squandered.

Wasted time is the time that is spent on activities or people that do not add value, true benefit or edification to your life or the life of others. It is unprofitable. It is unproductive. The Bible warns us many times about the consequences of wasting time. In the book of Proverbs, we find that lack, poverty, and idleness that leads to sin are all named among the residuum of time that has been wasted.

The bandit of Procrastination robs us of our precious time. It is opposition to our aspirations and goals, the saboteur of our very Purpose and must be avoided. Disorder and Laziness are the parents of procrastination because it is born out of misplaced priorities and a lazy character. We don't seem to mind admitting to others that we tend to procrastinate, but we do not want to admit that we are in fact lazy in some (if not all) areas of our lives. Why do we put things off? Why do we fail to do things until the last possible moment? Do you ever wonder how God must feel about how we spend the time that He has given us?

When we are wasting time, we are not fulfilling our purpose, pursuing any of our dreams or achieving any of the goals that we have set for ourselves. The more we procrastinate, the more we postpone the successful fulfillment of Purpose. Our desire should be to give to the world every ounce of greatness that God has placed inside of us – for His Glory - while we have this lifetime.

I sense that this is another opportunity to confess, so here goes…I have historically been a notorious procrastinator. I would say what I was going to do with my mouth but very rarely follow through with it. I would find all kinds of valueless things to spend my valuable time on. Making no progress toward Purpose (actually avoiding it). Being of no true benefit. At times, I felt as if there was just so much in me that I wanted to do that I didn't know where to start, so I chose to do what was comfortable – nothing. The problem with those choices was that my potential was never reached, and all that was locked up inside of me remained behind the bars of my consistent procrastination. Months turned to years and years turned to decades. I suddenly realized that time was not standing still to wait for me to get myself together. I finally got tired of myself. Tired of never finishing anything that I started. Tired of being regretful. Tired of knowing that I should be doing more but not being motivated enough to do it. Tired of being distracted. Tired of feeling unfulfilled. Just tired of being tired. So, I simply decided that I wanted my destined Purpose. To get it, I had to stop procrastinating and making excuses. So, just in case, My Love, you one day find yourself falling into that same comfortably unproductive state of idleness, I want to share with you the practical tactics that I used to defeat the enemy of procrastination in my life:

Establish Order, Daily. In 1 Corinthians chapter 14, Paul instructs God's people on how to keep order during their worship services. He states that God is not the author of confusion and that all things should be done decently and in order. If God desires decency and order in His corporate house of worship, He also desires them for our personal lives. For we are the temple of God according to 1 Corinthians 3:16.

Many of us have a myriad of things that we need to or want to get done in a day and life can often get chaotic and overwhelming if things are not kept in perspective. Writing down your vision for the day in a prioritized list is a definite way to set things in order. The key word being "prioritized"; remembering that God's order for our lives is: God first, Family next, then our Neighbors (church, community, etc.). When we get our priorities misplaced, it is a reflection of what and who we value more. We must keep the areas of our lives in their proper order.

Visible lists help to ensure that we are progressing forward towards our purpose and our goals. They keep us on task.

You must make time to write the list. At the end of your day, after you have settled in and relaxed is a great time to think about what you want to get accomplished the next day and write it down in order of importance, remembering God's order. Even if there are too many tasks on the list to achieve in one day, list them just the same. If the task does not get done the first day, carry it over to the top of the next day's list. I have found that writing a daily vision is an absolute must to combat chronic procrastination.

Eliminate Time Wasters. Omit excessive activities and counterproductive people that are not adding value, benefit or edification to your life. We all have them.

Technology. Mobile phones. Tablets. Computers. IPads. Today's technical apparatuses are ingenious. We can surf the web, play games, shop, record, watch TV/videos, communicate with others via text, email or video, take pictures, do our banking, and even take a college course all in the palm of our hand. We have the world at our fingertips. New social media sights and applications are being launched almost faster than we can keep up. Any spare moment we have can be fully occupied with these widgets.

<u>Television.</u> We can sit on the throne of our couch and call for the court jesters of our favorite movies and shows to come forth and entertain us with the simple wave of our royal scepter of a remote. 62 and 72-inch screens with 500 to 600 satellite channels keep our minds in a trance for hours at a time. Ridiculous.

Please do not think that I am against these brilliant inventions. I genuinely appreciate them. They serve their purpose when utilized befittingly, but they can most certainly become our greatest distractors and time wasters when used in excess.

<u>Busy work.</u> All of those activities that we involve ourselves in that do nothing but keep us occupied away from what we should be doing. Stop it.

<u>People.</u> Our friends and family can also waste our precious time if we fail to set boundaries in our relationships that protect it.

We must discipline ourselves against unbeneficial, disadvantageous, worthless habitudes.

Keep Yourself Motivated. If you are anything like me - prone to distraction, disheveled by discouragement, and intimidated by difficulty – then you, My Love, must be very intentional with your sources of motivation. One way to do so is to post your written goals in areas where you will see them and be reminded of them every day. And not only see them but say them. As I am writing this work, I have the words "Published Author" taped to my bathroom mirror so that each time I stand there, I can see my goal directly above the reflection of my head. It reminds me – every day. Very intentional.

Encourage yourself by speaking affirmatively over your life and your goals. The Bible teaches us that death and life are in the power of the tongue (Prov. 18:21). Get rid of the negative language we often use such as "I can't"… or "I'm never going to"….Change your monologue to start with "I will be a….", "I am…..", and "I can…" Speak positive affirmations of God's promises. Put your Purpose in the atmosphere! Say what God says about you, My Love. Say it often. Say it confidently. Say it until you see it. Do things, listen to things, watch things, read things and connect with things that correlate with your Purpose as often as you can.

Let Others Motivate You. Create for yourself an inner circle of like-minded people who have Purpose, goals, aspirations and vision like you do. Give them permission to tell you the bold truth and hold you accountable. Pray for and seek out a mentor (or two or three) from whom you can receive wise counsel, teaching, and guidance in the way of your Purpose. Naysayers, doubters, complainers, scoffers, pessimists, and skeptics should be far outside of your inner circle of colleagues. They will discourage you, distract you and zap the very energy from you. Love them, do good to them, minister to them whenever the Lord gives you the opportunity to, but no more. As long as they choose to exist in the negative, they are detrimental to your Purpose, and you cannot afford to be derailed.

Remain Focused. Do not get knocked off course by distractions or tedious life circumstances. Keep your focus on what is important: Purpose. Do not let failures deter you. When reaching for Purpose, you may have some unsuccessful attempts. You will surely face some opposition. The interviewer may decline your application, prospects may reject your business services, a company may refuse to publish your book, or some doors you attempt to walk through may close in your face. Those things happen on the road to Purpose. Stay focused on your goal despite setbacks or disappointments. There are some life situations and circumstances that arise unexpectedly and require our attention. They are unavoidable. Give them the attention they need and get back on course. It's ok to make a pit stop, but do not detour!

Ephesians 5: 15-16 admonishes us to live purposefully and make the most use of the time that we have. These realistic practices implemented into your everyday life will bring victory over the enemy of procrastination and help you to move consistently toward what God has designed for you.

*****

Prayer: Heavenly Father, thank you for your patience with me. Please forgive me for my slothfulness and idle ways. I will endeavor to do my best at everything that I do because all that I do, I do ultimately in service to you. Thank you for blessing my path as I go. In Jesus' name, Amen.

CHAPTER XIII

THE OMEGA
God, the Perfect Ending

O the depth of the riches both of the wisdom and knowledge of God! How unsearchable are his judgments, and his ways past finding out! For who hath known the mind of the Lord? Or who hath been his counselor? Or who hath first given to him, and it shall be recompensed unto him again? For of him, and through him, and to him, are all things: to whom be glory forever. Amen.
Romans 11:33-36

*****

My desire is to die empty
With nothing left undone in me
Having given all back to you
Having done all you have assigned me to do
With a heart that loved you wholly
With a soul that longed for you only
Lord, prepare me for that day
Please keep me in your straight and narrow way

That day when I shall surely see your face
I live simply to hear you say
"Ye shall be with Me in Paradise this day."

*****

God is Omega - the End. Like the two words
that close our favorite children's books: The End.
Story over. Nothing follows. After the story of our
life is over, God will be there. When these mortal
bodies live no more, God will be waiting for our
souls. If you have lived a life of faith in the Lord
Jesus, He will welcome you into the Eternal Rest
and Paradise of Heaven. If you chose to deny
Jesus and reject His gift of salvation, He will
banish you from His presence into the Eternal
Damnation of hell's fire. It will be one or the other
– paradise or torment, for eternity. You will either
hear Him say "Well done, thou good and faithful
servant. Enter ye into the Joy of the Lord" or
"Depart from me, ye worker of iniquity. I never
knew you". God is all that matters in the end. That
is what the focus text for this chapter says *"For of*

him, and through him, and to him, are all things…" In the end, we will all go back to God. The God of all Glory. We shall surely behold Him, face to face.

There are those who believe that there is no heaven or hell. Some believe that once we close our eyes on this side of forever, we simply cease to exist. Some believe that we get to live all over again, reincarnated as another person or thing. Some believe that we continue to roam the earth as invisible beings or spirits. People have varying beliefs about what happens to our souls after this life is over – the afterlife. One thing is certain, there is an eternity, and it is forever, neverending and everlasting. You must decide, My Love, where your soul will spend it. I read a bumper sticker on the back of a vehicle years ago that I never forgot. It said, "If you are living your life like there is no God, you'd better be right!" Funny, but so very true. Once death calls, it will be too late to speculate or wonder what happens next. You need to be sure while you live.

Our choice today is still as simple as it was in the days of the biblical Old Testament when God's prophet Moses declared the Word of the Lord to the children of Israel as they traveled in the wilderness towards the Promised Land. Along the way, their faith began to fail them. They began to doubt God because their path was not an easy one. The wilderness was not comfortable. It was a valley experience for the people of God. Instead of suffering well, they chose to complain and turn away from God. They began to set their affections on false idols and graven images. Through their leader, Moses, God said,

> *"I call heaven and earth to record this day against you, that I have set before you life and death, blessing and cursing: therefore choose life, that both thou and thy seed may live:* Deuteronomy 30:19

Elijah presented the same options to God's people after they had possessed the Promised Land and established kings to rule. Their king at one time was King Ahab, and his queen was the wicked Jezebel, who had deceived and influenced the children of Israel with the false gods of Baal and idol worship. Through the prophet Elijah, God said,

> *"How long halt ye between two opinions? If the Lord be God, follow him: but if Baal, then follow him…"* 1Kings 18:21.

Today we have the same choice to make as the children of Israel did well over 2,000 years ago – Eternal life or Eternal damnation. A life of blessings or a life that is cursed.

In these days that you are living in, My Love, just as it was in the days of Ahab and Jezebel, there is much to deceive you. Many false idol gods. Many people and things to steal your attention and entice you to seek after them rather than God. Money, careers, lovers, leaders, fame – they all have the potential to seduce you into worshipping them. Beware, My Love. The Bible says there are many men and women lurking among us in sheep's clothing, claiming to know and hear from God to gain our trust. But they are in fact ravening wolves, ready to pounce on our lives and sink their lying fangs into our faith. Titus 1:16 says "*They profess that they know God; but in works they deny him, being abominable, and disobedient, and unto every good work reprobate.*" Though their words profess Christ, their actions consistently deny God. They live lives of deceit that are contrary to His Word. Be careful of those who take the truths of God and twist them just slightly enough to fit their sinful, deceitful agenda. They are in search of vain glory, filthy lucre, and their intentions are pure evil.

Now more than ever, people are turning away from God and following after their fleshly desires, disregarding the standards of God's righteousness and doing whatever feels good to them yet still calling themselves lovers of God. They lie. "You only live once" is the motto of this world. "Do whatever feels right to you" is the standard by which this society lives.

Men and women are lusting after undeserved positions with false qualifications. They vie for the "title" of the evangelist, pastor, bishop, and prophet, ignorant of the fact that those are not titles, but holy offices, to which only God can effectively appoint. Their pride and arrogance push them into competitive behaviors to be seen and idolized by people. They have no desire to please God. They crave attention and thrive off of the praise and admiration of man. They seek the glory that belongs to God alone. And so, the Lord's sacred pulpit is being used as a platform to promote frivolous things like how to be wealthy and successful according to the standards of this world. These wolves promote the love of money and boast about the amount of material things they have. They get people excited and emotional with the volumes and inflections of their voice but will not use it to sound the alarm against sin and its consequences because they themselves are living lives of sin. And as a result, congregations upon congregations of people are being led astray and left to face the everlasting doom of a burning hell because the real truth of God's Word is scarcely being taught. These false prophets speak only what sounds good, what makes the people feel good, and what makes them look good.

This is why you must study the Word of God. Read and study the Bible. I admonish you to know the truth for yourself, My Love, so you will not be *"…tossed to and fro, and carried about with every wind of doctrine, by the sleight of men, and cunning craftiness, whereby they lie in wait to deceive"* as described in Ephesians 4:14. When you have knowledge of God and His Word for yourself, you will not be easily deceived by the charisma and eloquent speech of those who come to beguile you. God warns us over and over in His Word about these false prophets:

> Matt 7:15 – *"Beware the false prophets, which come to you in sheep's clothing, but inwardly they are ravening wolves."*
> Jer 14:14 – *"Then the Lord said unto me, the prophets prophesy lies in my name: I sent them not, neither have I commanded them, neither spake unto them: they prophesy unto you a false vision and divination, and a thing of nought, and the deceit of their heart."*
> Matt 24:11 & 24 – *"And many false prophets shall rise, and shall deceive many…For many shall arise false Christs, and false prophets, and shall shew great signs and wonders; insomuch that, if it were possible, they shall deceive the very elect."*
> 2Pet 2:1 – *"But there were false prophets also among the people, even as there shall be false teachers among you, who privily shall bring in damnable heresies, even denying the Lord that bought them, and bring upon themselves swift destruction."*
> 1John 4:1 – *"Beloved, believe not every spirit, but try the spirits whether they are of God: because many false prophets are gone out into the world."*

Though many deny Him now, the Bible declares in Romans 14:11 that the day will surely come when every knee shall bow to the Lord, and every tongue shall confess to Him. The question is when will you choose to bow? Will it be now while His enduring grace and tender mercies are waiting with loving kindness to receive your worship unto everlasting life? Or will it be when He comes with wrath to address the sin and wickedness of this world with judgment and the fire of eternal damnation?

My eternal brother told a story one evening as he taught Bible study of a young man who had committed a crime and was appointed a lawyer by the court. The lawyer admonished him not to leave town because he was confident that he would be able to argue the young man's case successfully, and that the judge would find him not guilty. But the young man knew that he was guilty in his heart and did not believe there was any way that the lawyer was going to be able to win his case. So he fled. Years later, the young man wanted to come back to his home. So he purposed to find the lawyer and explain that he had left all those years earlier because he was scared, but he was ready now to have the lawyer plead his case before the judge and have the charges erased. He eventually found the lawyer and made his appeal. But the lawyer answered him and said, "If you would have stayed when I asked you to, I could have helped you and gotten the charges against you erased; but now, it is too late. For I am no longer the lawyer, I am the judge."

The time is coming when the Lord Jesus will return to this earth. He will not come as the meek and humble servant He was when He walked the earth over two millenniums ago, nor as the lovingly gracious Advocate He has been for us

since His resurrection and ascension back to Glory. But He shall return as the Righteous Judge to pour out His wrath and judgment upon this sinfully wicked earth, and all those who chose to reject Him. The time for repentance will have passed. Mercy will be no more. Earth will suffer the wrath of God, and there will be no one who will deny the Power of the Almighty. Every knee will willingly bow in reverence to the God of All Glory.

God is calling you to Him while you still have time, My Love. He's asking you not to run from His saving grace as the young man in the story did. It doesn't matter what you've done. He knows all about it and loves you in spite of it all. Come to Jesus while He is your Advocate and let Him erase your charges, wash all of your sins away and give you a Happily Ever After in Eternal Glory with Him.

In the end, when the story of this life is over, we will see Him, God the Omega, face to face. What will you hear Him say, My Love?

*****

Prayer: Heavenly Father, thank you for the gift of this life. I acknowledge you as the Author and Finisher of it, the Alpha of its beginning and the Omega of its ending. You are allowing me the opportunity to choose which course I will take. Help me to consistently follow the straight and narrow way to Eternal Life with you. In your son Jesus' name, Amen.

AFTERWORD

As I close this letter, I have one final question for you to consider: If Death came for you at this moment, do you know for sure where you would spend eternity? If you are unsure, God is giving you the opportunity to be sure, right now. Nothing written on the previous pages matters at all if you do not know the Lord Jesus as your personal Savior. God only requires that we believe in Jesus Christ, His death and resurrection with our heart and confess our belief with our mouth. Romans 10:9-10 says *"That if thou shalt confess with thy mouth the Lord Jesus, and shalt believe in thine heart that God hath raised him from the dead, thou shalt be saved. For with the heart man believeth unto righteousness; and with the mouth confession is made unto salvation."* If you believe that with all sincerity, say this out loud…

Dear God, I come to you confessing that I am a sinner. I want to be in right relationship with you.
I am sorry for my sins and the life that I have lived.
Please forgive me.
With my heart, I believe that you gave your only son Jesus to die for my sins; that He shed His precious blood on the cross at Calvary and gave His life for me; that you raised Him from the dead, and He sits at your right hand in Glory. This very moment, I ask you to come into my heart as my personal Savior and help me to live for you.
Thank you for saving me.
Amen.

Welcome to NEW LIFE in Christ!
Seal it with your signature below as a sign that you are in covenant relationship with God.

_____   _____

Your signature   Date

If you've prayed this prayer, please email us at
flowingfrommyheart@outlook.com and share your testimony.

ABOUT THE AUTHOR

Verjuana Foreman is an energetically fun-loving wife and mother who loves King Jesus with all of her heart, soul, and might. Her passions in life are her Amazing Husband, seven gorgeous daughters, and two precious granddaughters. She has been favored to serve her country as a non-commissioned officer in the United States Army; as well as serve her community as an entrepreneur and writer. She considers herself truly blessed to be able to serve others through business and authorship, and gratefully looks forward to the doors of opportunity that the Lord will open for her and her family.

Other titles available:

Flowing From My Heart

THE JOURNAL

A Journal By
V. R. FOREMAN

Available in print on www.Amazon.com.

Coming 2016:

HOW MAY I HELP YOU?

THE LOST AND DYING ART OF CUSTOMER SERVICE

A Manual By

V. R. FOREMAN

Will be available on www.Amazon.com in print and Kindle edition.

www.ingramcontent.com/pod-product-compliance
Lightning Source LLC
LaVergne TN
LVHW011334080426
835513LV00006B/342